Classroom Routines That Really Work for PreK and Kindergarten

by Kathleen Hayes and Reneé Creange

SCHOLASTIC PROFESSIONAL BOOKS

New York • Toronto • London • Auckland • Sydney
Mexico City • New Delhi • Hong Kong • Buenos Aires

Dedication

For Jodie, David, and Mary whose love and support
made this book possible.   —KH

For my daughters, Cara and Elissa; the teachers and
children at the Teaneck Community Charter School;
and a wise mentor, Margot Hammond.   —RC

Front cover design by Joni Holst

Interior design by Sydney Wright

Cover photograph and photographs on pages 17, 32, 39, 65, and 89 by Nina Roberts.

All others courtesy of Kathleen Hayes.

Illustrations on pages 117-120 by Maxie Chambliss.

ISBN 0-590-02928-2

Contents

Foreword

Even the best student teaching cannot diminish the anxiety most new teachers feel when they are assigned to their very first class. And although veteran teachers have experience working in their favor, they too face anxiety-provoking moments in their careers; for example, when they change grade levels or decide their teaching needs a jumpstart. This stress can be especially real for those teaching pre-kindergarten or kindergarten because to four- and five-year-olds, the teacher is supposed to have everything under control.

But because of reforms in public education, new teachers are often not given time to learn in their first year, as they once were—and veteran teachers, it's assumed, don't need the time. This means teachers at all experience levels are not free to try out ideas that may be crucial to their success, such as setting up learning centers, managing the classroom, scheduling the day, and incorporating content-area standards into lesson plans—everything that goes into creating effective learning environments. Frequently, it is the routine tasks that drive our best and brightest away from the profession. With *Classroom Routines That Really Work for Pre-K and Kindergarten*, Kathleen Hayes and Reneé Creange provide preventative medicine. It is the ultimate "how to" book.

Too often, the colleague down the hall does not have the time or energy to share her secrets. These authors are more generous. They tell all about creating a balanced approach to literacy for young children, monitoring learning centers, introducing new materials for use in centers, displaying and using books, interacting positively with parents, and, most important, organizing that six-and-a-half-hour day.

The book is filled with examples from the Newark public schools where Kathleen has worked as a facilitator for the New Beginnings Project, a staff-development initiative with The Bank Street College of Education. Kathleen and Reneé show precisely the routines that are turning our pre-K and kindergarten classrooms into environments where students thrive as learners.

When I was a principal, one of my responsibilities was to support new and experienced teachers on their journeys to becoming the teachers they wanted to be. To do that, I had to help each one design a program that took a year to complete. It was a lot of work. We could've used *Classroom Routines That Really Work*. It would've helped us avoid a lot of the frustrations that diminish our effectiveness as educators—and to engage in practices that ensure success for all.

Gayle W. Griffin, Ph.D.
Associate Superintendent, Department of Teaching and Learning
Newark Public Schools

Acknowledgments

We want to thank all the teachers we've worked with at Project New Beginnings, a collaboration between Bank Street College and Newark, New Jersey, Public Schools. Bank Street representatives provide Newark's early childhood teachers with support to help them create developmentally appropriate classrooms. We've worked with teachers as they've struggled to create classrooms where children feel respected and valued for who they are and what they can do. In turn, they've helped us to modify our ideas to meet the needs of their diverse groups. We've also learned much from the faculty and children of the Teaneck Community Charter School, a school where teachers and parents work collaboratively to develop responsive classrooms. And, of course, the Bank Street School for Children's faculty members and students, who have taught us so much about how children learn.

In particular, we want to thank Lenore Furman, a kindergarten teacher at Abington Avenue Elementary School in Newark, New Jersey. This book contains so many of her techniques and routines, as well as signs and charts that she uses with her students. Her classroom is a place where children's questions are encouraged, where their work is valued, and where, together with their teachers, they create a loving community where it is safe to take risks and grow as learners. Lenore is a gifted educator who thinks long and hard about what she does and why she does it. "Thanks" does not begin to express our gratitude for all she's given to us and to this project.

We can't end without thanking Raymond Coutu, our editor at Scholastic, and Elisabeth Jakab, our editor at Bank Street College, who provided gentle encouragement, consistent support, and the push we needed to write this book.

Introduction

Classroom Routines That Really Work was written to help pre-K and kindergarten teachers establish classroom routines that foster a sense of security, community, and joy among children. We hope our ideas and suggestions will inspire both new and experienced teachers to discover ways to design environments where children truly feel at home.

We have created, and have worked with other teachers who have created, classrooms where students engage in a variety of open-ended activities, in imaginative ways. Although these classrooms may seem to run themselves, we always take an active role in establishing underlying structures that allow children to take risks and grow.

In the book, we follow children through a typical day's schedule, while discussing how things change over the course of the school year. We begin at the beginning: setting up the classroom environment. You'll find suggestions to help you create a classroom where students can function independently, as well as ways to introduce yourself to the children and their parents even before the first day.

Helping children overcome separation anxiety as they transition to school requires special work. How you plan for and implement routines during the first weeks can help children cope with separation, so we provide tips for creating a schedule that not only meets the requirements of your curriculum, but the needs of your children as well. We describe ways to help children quickly feel that they belong.

As the school year proceeds, students typically become more comfortable in their classroom, but separating from home can continue to be stressful. We provide examples of different types of arrival-time activities that help children transition easily into the classroom, on a day-to-day basis.

Helping young children learn to talk together—to share ideas and listen to one another—can be a daunting task. Therefore, we offer strategies for creating whole-group meetings that give children opportunities to engage in conversations with you and with each other, in ways that build community and allow you to introduce new materials and ideas to the children.

But if students are to have a voice in your classroom, they need to be given choices about how they spend their time there. To accomplish this, we suggest dividing your room into centers, designated areas for engaging in different kinds of work. We give you ideas for setting up centers, introducing them to children, and supporting the work that's carried out there. We also include ways to assess and record what the children are doing, so that you can extend their work and thinking.

Although it is important to give students choice, it's also important to make sure they get effective direct instruction as well. That's why we have included ways to organize and structure small-group work times, when children partake in literacy, math, science, and social studies activities under your careful guidance.

In addition to small-group instruction, there are times in the day when you will want to provide instruction to the whole group. Creating these moments throughout the day requires careful thought and planning. So we offer practical ideas for keeping all students engaged and on task.

The book also contains suggestions for meeting children's basic needs for nourishment and rest. Preparing healthy snacks, sharing them "family style," and making time for real rest energizes children and helps them feel motivated throughout the day.

Finding time and ways to help students engage in safe, open-ended outdoor activities is critical for young children, too. Here, you'll find advice on helping children play together, as well as information for explaining to parents and administrators why outdoor play is so important to the developing child.

Throughout the book we talk about why it's important to create routines for students, but we also recognize that variety can be the spice of life. That's why special events are important. Whether you're celebrating the completion of a theme study, the birthday of a child, or a national holiday, there are ways to keep the time low-key and fun for all—even you! You'll find them here.

As the day comes to an end, it's easy for chaos to rule. Everyone is tired, and there are always so many loose ends to tie up. We've created guidelines that will help you establish an end-of-the-day routine that eases the children out the door and gives you the opportunity to communicate with parents.

Before you know it, the end of the year approaches. After spending months together, and feeling very much at home in their classroom, students will need your help in saying goodbye. In the final chapter, you will find ways to celebrate accomplishments and talk to the children in ways that provide the emotional support they need to move on.

As we worked on this book project, we scoured our own files and consulted many excellent teachers of young children. We hope that our ideas, suggestions, and classroom routines will help you create imaginative, enriching, and emotionally safe classrooms where community is built and celebrated.

KH–RC

Chapter 1

Beginning the School Year

For young children, going to school can be exciting and frightening, exhilarating and exhausting. They usually ask themselves lots of questions: What will my classroom look like? How will I find it? Will there be a safe place for my things? Will my teacher like me?

For the parents of young children, the start of the school year can also be worrisome. They have their own questions: Will the teachers understand my child? Will they give her what she needs? Will I have the chance to speak with them regularly? Is the school safe in every sense?

How effectively you help children and parents "move into" the classroom—how quickly they're made to feel at home there—often determines how successful that crucial first month will be. Here are some ways to jumpstart your relationships.

HOME VISITS

Some administrators encourage teachers of young children to make home visits prior to the start of the school year; others require it.

To arrange a home visit, telephone each student's parent or primary caregiver to introduce yourself and schedule a time that works for everyone. "Hello, I'm Jane Scott, Zachary's new teacher," a teacher might say. "I'm looking forward to having him in my class. If possible, I'd like to meet him before school begins. I've found that visiting each of my students before the year begins makes the start of school easier. I'm calling to see what might be a good day and time to visit you and Zachary. I will only stay for about a half hour."

During the home visit, take your cue from the child. Some children may be willing to interact with you, while others may not. If he is outgoing, you might want to encourage him to show you his room, his favorite toys, or any pets he might have.

If the child doesn't want to talk to you, that's fine, too. Bringing a small gift might help to break the ice. Books are always a good choice. Reading with the child during the visit establishes an early bond between the two of you, and the book itself serves as a lasting reminder of your visit.

It is also a great way to learn more about each child's reading readiness. Is she familiar with books? Does

Teacher Tip

Open a Book, Connect With a Child

Looking for inexpensive, quality paperbacks to bring to home visits? Book clubs are a good source. Select simple, accessible picture books, ones the child might not already own. Some titles to consider are:

- *Umbrella* by Taro Yashima. A young girl walks to preschool with her new umbrella and, for the first time, doesn't need to hold her parent's hand.

- *Mr. Gumpy's Outing* by John Burningham. Children and animals travel together, helping one another out, until they arrive safely back home.

- *Where Can It Be?* by Ann Jonas. A young boy has lost something, but we don't discover what it is until the last page.

- *The Line-Up Book* by Marisabina Russo. Sam's mom calls him to lunch, but he'd rather line his toys up from his bedroom to the kitchen. When his mother sees what's taking him so long, she recognizes his work.

- *Corduroy* by Don Freeman. A classic tale of a bear that gets lost, struggles to make sense of his new environment, and eventually finds a friend who makes him feel at home.

she help turn pages? Does she know the story? Does she get excited about other stories she knows?

Finally, by sharing a book with the child, she will associate you with other adults who might already be reading to her. The child starts viewing you as someone she can trust. And for those children whose parents don't read to them, your read-aloud might serve as a model to them.

Bringing homemade play dough to a home visit is another way to trigger interaction between you and the child. (See Chapter 5, page 41 for the recipe.) You might explain that you will be using the dough at school, and give the recipe to his parents so they can make it together at home. Forging even a small link like this often eases the child's fears. He now not only knows what you look and act like, but also what he will find at school. You've unveiled part of its great mystery.

We've used children's photographs to label cubbies, attendance charts, birthday graphs, and so forth—and have often taken those photographs during home visits. If you bring a camera with you, the child may be willing to be photographed. After all, having their picture taken is a familiar and frequent activity in most children's lives. But some children may be shy. If that's the case, tell her how you intend to use the picture. She may consent. But if she doesn't, don't insist. Simply ask her parents if they can spare a snapshot.

Introductory Letters

If your school or center has a parent handbook, mail it to families or bring it to the home visit. If it doesn't, compose a letter introducing yourself and your colleagues, explaining your procedures for making children feel comfortable. It might look something like the sample on page 12.

If you can't make home visits, or if family members discourage visits, a letter like this can be mailed out as soon as you get a class list.

If you hand deliver the letter during the home visit, and you have limited time, try to resist talking in detail about it with parents, since your purpose for being there is to bond with the child. If you do have time to talk, though, the letter will serve as a handy reminder of your conversation.

Welcome to Room 204!

All of us, head teacher Kathleen, full-time assistant Anna, and part-time student teacher David, are eager to welcome you and your child to our school. To help ease the transition from home to school, we have some suggestions:

■ Please bring a complete set of extra clothes, in case of toileting accidents. Be sure each piece is clearly marked with your child's name.

■ Give your child a family picture to bring to school. He can keep it in his cubby or a pocket. It will be reassuring for him to be able to "see" you during the first weeks of school.

■ We will have a rest period every day at school. Your child may bring a small blanket and a soft toy for use during rest period. If you have any questions about the kind of toy your child should bring, feel free to contact one of us.

■ Many children experience difficulty separating from parents in the morning. If your child is one of them, please let us know so that we can help her deal with those painful goodbyes.

■ If, after a particularly difficult separation, you want us to call you during the day and let you know how your child is doing, we will. Please make sure you leave a phone number where you can be reached.

■ For your child's safety, please let us know, as soon as possible, who will be picking him up at the end of each day. This information will be posted on the bulletin board by the classroom door.

■ Although we are all eager to talk with you about your child, the morning arrival period is not always the best time for a lengthy discussion. The children need our attention, and we want to be available to them. But, please, feel free to call the school at [school's phone number] and leave a message or e-mail us at [your e-mail address]. We will get back to you as soon as possible.

There will be an orientation meeting for parents on [date and time of meeting here]. The school will provide child care if you need it. The meeting should last only an hour. We hope you are able to join us.

Sincerely,
Kathleen Hayes, Anna Lewis, and David Small

You can also mail an introductory letter or postcard to each child in your class before school begins. The sample postcard on page 13 was written to incoming four- and five-year-olds at the Bank Street School for Children.

Hello Hannah:

My name is Kathleen, and I will be one of your teachers this fall. Anna and David will be your other teachers. We are busy getting Room 204 ready for you and the other children. We have a rabbit named Sam Hopper, some fish, and lots of toys you can play with during the day. I like to sing and play my guitar, and I love teaching four- and five-year-olds! I was at the beach this summer. It was a lot of fun. What did you do this summer?

We are all eager to get to know you. See you soon!

Kathleen

Classroom Visits

Inviting parents and children into the classroom as you're setting it up is another way to make them feel at home before the school year begins. Try to arrange to have all families visit on the same day, a week or so before school's official start date. Call each one and suggest a twenty-minute slot during which they can visit. Don't schedule more than three families at a time. And allow at least ten minutes between groups in case you have stragglers or need to catch a breath.

Classroom visits give you an opportunity to introduce yourself, show the children and their parents the classroom, and point out where each child will put personal things. They are also a terrific way to start introducing the children to each other. Early first-hand exposure like this can greatly ease the anxiety that often accompanies the first days of school.

Teacher Tip

Set Up for Classroom Visits

Before the children and their parents visit your classroom, make sure you:

■ Tag cubbies with the children's names.

■ Label spots on the wall where student artwork will be displayed.

■ Post a sign outside the door that indicates who "lives" in this classroom. List all the children's names.

■ Hang an attendance chart with every child's name.

■ Mark other places with children's names, where appropriate.

Personalizing the space this way makes it clear that you are expecting every child and that there are places throughout the room just for him or her.

It's a good idea to have things to play with during visits. For younger children, provide materials that might be familiar to them from daycare, preschool, or home. For older children, provide materials that they may recognize from earlier school experiences. Possibilities include:

* Beads for stringing
* Puzzles, both simple and challenging
* Legos and/or Duplos
* Table blocks
* Books that may be familiar, as well as some new ones
* Crayons, jumbo colored pencils, paper
* Play dough, cookie cutters, and rollers
* Dolls, doll clothes, briefcases, bags, and dress-up items such as shirts and hats
* Jumbo Cusinaire rods

Each item should have a home—a shelf space, drawer, or container—that is clearly labeled with its picture.

Provide Open-Ended Materials

With materials that encourage free play, children are in control of what they create, which satisfies their natural curiosity to innovate and problem solve.

At the beginning of the year, it's best to provide only a few kinds of open-ended materials, but a generous supply of them. This enables children to work together in small groups comfortably, without having to compete over limited quantities for very particular types of activities. They stand a better chance of learning about and from one another. A child who is unfamiliar with Legos, for instance, will discover how to use them by observing what more experienced children do.

For each item, clearly label its container and the shelf on which it goes.

Setting Up Your Classroom

A well-ordered classroom takes a great deal of thought and energy. The time it takes, however, is worth it. In a well-ordered classroom, children find things more easily and return them to their rightful places. Carrying out such tasks independently empowers them and fosters a feeling of belonging. As you arrange your classroom for early visits, as well as for that all-important first day of school, keep these suggestions in mind:

★ Position shelves and tables so that they don't create "runways." Long, narrow passages tempt children to run, posing a risk to them and the group.

★ Put tall furniture against walls so that you can see what's happening in every corner of the room.

★ Use shelves to define areas for block building, dramatic play, and other activities. Well-defined spaces promote thoughtful work.

★ Situate the meeting area and library corner away from noisy areas.

★ Store books in bins or bookshelves that are low enough for children to reach.

★ Place your listening center equipment, including tape and CD players, headphones, and book/tape sets, in or near your library corner.

★ Place drawing and writing materials in a central location, so children can access them easily from any area of room.

★ Position the sand/water and art tables near the sink.

★ Store manipulatives on shelves in your meeting area. That way, the meeting area can double as a space for building with manipulatives during work time.

Teacher Tip

Create a Well-Ordered Classroom With These Resources

Check out this book and video for more information about room arrangement:

The Creative Curriculum for Early Childhood, Third Edition, by Diane Trister Dodge and Laura J. Colker.

The New Room Arrangement as a Teaching Strategy (video) by Diane Trister Dodge.

Both can be ordered from Teaching Strategies by calling 1-800-637-3652 or visiting www.teachingstrategies.com.

Parent Orientation Meeting

The more access parents have to the school during the initial weeks, the more comfortable they'll feel about leaving their children there. Early home and classroom visits can help significantly. You might also want to hold an orientation meeting during the first week of school to give parents a chance to learn more about you, the school day, and the classroom environment. Because many parents work during the day, you may get a better turn-out if you hold the meeting in the evening.

In addition to learning about you and your teaching, parents can get quick and clear answers to questions that were not answered completely during the home or school visit, or new ones they may have. This event is important. Consider it your first step in establishing regular and healthy communication with parents.

At the orientation meeting, you might want to:

★ Introduce yourself. Tell parents things about yourself that will reassure them, such as how long you've been teaching, why you teach, and anything else that will make them trust you and make you "real" to them.

★ Review the material you gave them during the home visit or sent them by mail.

★ Give them a copy of a typical daily schedule to show them exactly what their child is doing during the day.

★ Explain how and under what circumstances you will contact them, and provide guidelines for contacting you.

★ Allow significant time for their questions.

Communicate With Families

Staying in touch with parents is key. Here are a few ways to maintain regular contact.

■ Send home a brief newsletter each week describing what happened in class and listing any upcoming events, particularly those you would like parents to attend or participate in.

■ If your school has a voicemail system, record a weekly message containing exciting news and upcoming events. Parents can call the number, listen to the message, hang up, or leave a message if they need to. This reduces the need to send notes home.

■ If parents drop off and pick up their children, rather than a temporary caregiver, use that time to talk briefly to them about what's happening in class. If you need to discuss something in detail, arrange a meeting.

■ You might also post a calendar outside your classroom door. A simple one, made from an 18-by-24-inch piece of paper, can be used to promote events to which parents are invited. When the children are ready, you might want to give them the job of keeping the calendar, on a rotating basis.

Chapter 2

The First Few Weeks of School

I magine you've just landed in a foreign country. Can you find your way around? Does anything look familiar? Can you locate things easily? Do you have the words to ask questions that will help you find your way? Chances are, the answer is no.

For many young children, this is what going to school is like. Everything is new, different, and sometimes completely unrecognizable. Getting to know the school's environment and culture takes time. For some children, it can take days. For others, weeks. And for others, it can take more than a month.

From the first day of school, and throughout the initial weeks, establishing consistent and predictable classroom routines is the best way to make children feel confident and secure. Routines are a child's and a teacher's best friend.

The First Day of School

Welcoming the Children ☼

Let's start from the beginning: day one. Children react to their first day of school in different ways. Some are eager. Some are hesitant. Some have mixed emotions. It's important for you to tailor your welcome according to what the child brings. Here's how one kindergarten teacher, Lenore Furman of Abington Avenue Elementary in Newark, New Jersey, greeted a child who was experiencing some anxiety:

Jamie arrives at school with his grandmother. They walk down the long corridor and find Room Number 204. Jamie's grandmother points to a large white chart hanging outside the classroom door. On the chart is a column of words written in brightly colored magic marker. Jamie cannot read the chart, but his grandmother explains that it is a list of names of the children in the class. She finds Jamie's name and points it out to him with her index finger. The first letter is in red. The rest of the letters are in blue.

Ms. Furman opens the door and greets them warmly. She tells Jamie she is glad to see him and how much fun they are going to have. She also tells him that he is the only child in her class whose name starts with the letter *J*. She puts her finger on the same spot on the chart that his grandmother did and shows him the red *J*, running her finger over it to make the shape. She also informs Jamie that his name has been written in many places inside the classroom, too, and that he'll be able to find it simply by looking for the red *J*.

Once inside, Ms. Furman takes Jamie to a row of wooden cubbies with the children's names attached to them. Together, they look for the red *J*. When they find Jamie's cubby, Ms. Furman shows him the clothing hook and the two storage shelves inside. Jamie hangs his windbreaker on the hook and puts his lunchbox on the top shelf. His favorite action figure remains tightly clenched in his hand, however, which is fine with Ms. Furman. She leads him over to the attendance chart and shows him how to sign in. Jamie is now officially a student of Room 204. And, because of Ms. Furman's efforts, he feels a lot more at home than he did when he arrived.

Taking Attendance ☼

It's important for children to see some sort of visible indicator that they belong in your classroom. The indicator could be a list of names outside the door, as in Ms. Furman's case, or a display of photographs. It could also be an attendance chart. An attendance chart sends a powerful message to children: Knowing who's present and who's missing matters.

Interactive pocket charts are especially useful for taking attendance and building young children's reading skills. Choose a chart with enough pockets for each child in the class. Create a name card for each child and place it backwards in the chart. When the children arrive, they turn their cards to display their names, showing that they are in. As they leave, they turn the cards over to hide their names, showing that they are out. Children quickly learn where their cards are on the chart. Photographs can also be used on each pocket to make it easier for children to locate their cards, while also helping them to learn their classmates' names.

This interactive pocket chart signals whether children are in or out.

Attendance charts can be designed to resemble familiar objects, such as a schoolhouse with removable "window" cards, a fish bowl with "fish" cards, or a tree with "apple" cards, as shown on the next page.

This kind of chart, usually displayed on a large bulletin board, requires children to do a little more work. Upon arriving at school, they search through a bunch of laminated paper apples spread across a table, with the children's names on the front and Velcro tabs on the back. Once a child finds the apple with her name on it, she

takes it over to the tree. She then locates her name on a tree branch, which also has Velcro affixed to it, and attaches her apple to that spot. During the year, the children will learn to recognize their first names and match them quickly. You can add last names when the children are ready, to strengthen sight recognition of their whole names.

Exploring the Room

Lenore Furman's attendance chart helps children recognize their names and their classmates'.

After a child has added his name to the attendance chart, invite him to explore the room with his parent or caregiver. You could also invite him to a table to draw a design on a five-by-eight-inch index card, using crayons and jumbo-colored pencils. By attaching his drawing with clear contact paper to his cubby or above his coat hook, you give him another way to recognize where his things belong.

At another table, put out play dough and cookie cutters, rollers, and plastic knives. Children will appreciate this familiar activity on their first day of school. (See Chapter 5, page 41 for play dough recipe.) Since most of them will be drawn instantly to the dough, try to have an assistant teacher at the table, to help the children get to know one another as they play.

When all the children have arrived, have the teachers, aides, or adult volunteers circulate and encourage the children and their caregivers to explore the room at their own pace. After thirty to forty minutes, announce that clean-up will occur in five minutes.

After five minutes, give the clean-up signal and ask adults to help children put materials away. If your storage shelves and containers are labeled with drawings as well as words, all the children should be able to figure out quickly where things belong.

Separating from Caregivers

When it's time for parents to say goodbye, children often panic. Take Mary, for example. After she puts away the crayons, her mom gives her a reassuring kiss. Nonetheless, Mary instantly dissolves into tears. The teacher approaches her and says, "I know it's really hard to let your mom go to work, but she'll be back at the end of the day to pick you up. Would you like to give her the picture you drew so she can hang it up in her office?" Together, the teacher, Mary, and her mom go to the daily schedule to show Mary exactly when her mom will return.

Many children, like Mary, need gentle support from you to be able to say goodbye. In addition to the daily schedule, a photograph of family members, to keep in a pocket or a cubby, can be comforting to younger children. If you have a Polaroid camera, take a picture of each child with his caregiver on the first day. If a photograph isn't possible, and the child clearly needs reassurance, ask her caregiver for an object—a special pen, an inexpensive piece of jewelry, a change purse—that the child can keep until the end of the day. Objects like these will help the child feel connected.

If a child is seriously distressed by the separation, ask the caregiver for her phone number so you can call in case of emergency or with an update on how the child is doing. Remember, adults are often distressed by the separation, too.

Singing Your Way into Meeting

As children gravitate toward the meeting area, singing familiar songs can help speed up the process, since stragglers will most assuredly want to finish cleaning up so they can join in. At the beginning of the year, choose songs that most children will know, such as "Twinkle, Twinkle Little Star" or "Bah, Bah Black Sheep."

When everyone is settled in the meeting area, begin a new song, one that includes a child's name in the lyric. This is a surefire way to help children learn each other's names. The song should be fairly simple, such as:

> Jamie has a red shirt, red shirt, red shirt.
> Jamie has a red shirt on today.
> Sharon has blue pants, blue pants, blue pants.
> Sharon has blue pants on today.

Teacher Tip

Make Songs Your Own

Of the many excellent songbooks for children, it's hard to find a better one than *American Folk Songs for Children* by Ruth Seeger (Turtleback, 1948). In addition to containing the words and music to ninety of America's best-loved songs, it has a helpful introduction that explains how to modify songs to include children's names and respond to their ideas for new verses.

Some children will be eager to be center stage; others will want to wait a few days. So before choosing a child's name for a song, ask permission. If a child says no, that's fine. The other children learn that child's name nonetheless, because you've addressed her by name directly.

The Weeks Following the First Day

Establishing Classroom Routines and Rules

Morning meeting is a pivotal time because it gives children an opportunity to communicate, and it gives you an opportunity to introduce and reinforce routines and rules. During the first few weeks of school, keep meetings short. Present open-ended questions that all students can answer. You might ask, for example:

★ What do you think you'll play when we go outside today?

★ What do you think you'll do after school today?

★ How did you come to school this morning?

Many children will be eager to respond, but will have trouble waiting to be called on. Be gentle in reminding them to wait their turn. Encourage them to raise their hands before speaking. And, of course, some children may not be so eager. Reading from the "News of the Day" book might help to get those quieter children talking. (See Chapter 3, page 30.) But don't insist. It takes some children weeks before they are willing to speak up in a group.

Use morning meeting to review rules, such as how you would like children to go to the bathroom. Are they to carry a bathroom pass? Are they to go one at a time? Should they ask permission of the head teacher first? Whatever your rules, you must spell them out clearly on day one and review them until everyone understands and

Teacher Tip

Allow Time to Learn Routines

The first weeks of school are generally tough for young children because they have so many things to learn. Go slowly, and make sure that you and your assistants are always free to respond to children who aren't sure what to do. Remember, children want to please you. They want to do what you ask of them. But, in order for that to happen, you must tell them what you expect. They will learn the routines if you give them plenty of time and attention.

is following them. For more ideas about how to conduct a morning meeting, see Chapter 4.

Creating a Schedule That Children Can Use ☼

To help children learn their daily schedule, hang a set of cards on the wall, window, or bulletin board in the meeting area every morning, before the children arrive. On each card, draw a picture that represents one of the day's activities, and write the word for the activity below the picture. Make sure the cards are large enough so that the children can see them easily. (See Appendix for a sampling of reproducible cards.) Five-by-eight index cards generally work well. Once you have prepared the cards for all the day's activities, line them up in two columns, one for morning activities, and the other for afternoon activities. Attach them to a wall or window with Velcro, or to the bulletin board with thumbtacks. These schedule cards enable children to see at a glance what their day looks like, as well as the flow of activities.

By posting illustrated schedule cards each morning, this teacher gives her students a sense of what their day will look like.

Assigning Jobs ☼

If you want your students to feel powerful in their new classroom, they need to know that there are many things they can do on their own. In the first few weeks, they will have learned to store classroom materials and personal materials, use the attendance chart, and keep track of the day's schedule. These are important ways for students to take care of themselves, but they can also learn to take care of others. By creating jobs for them, you help children become responsible members of the group by contributing to the overall well being of the community. Here are some suggestions for a class of about twenty-five children.

Jobs for one child at a time:

- Electrician: Turns lights on and off when instructed by an adult.

- Counter: Puts a marble or other small counting device in a jar every morning, to keep track of the number of days since school began.

- Meteorologist: Draws a picture of the weather for posting on the weather chart.

- Calendar Person: Decides on and writes (or dictates) a significant event of the day for posting on the calendar.

- Class Comforter: Helps when a classmate needs support.

- Snail Custodian: Feeds and waters snails.

- Rabbit Caretaker: Feeds and waters rabbit.

- Fish Feeder: Feeds the fish.

- Clean-Up Announcer: Rings the clean-up signal.

- Line Leader: Leads the line when the class is moving through the building or on a trip.

- Caboose: Brings up the end of the line.

Jobs for up to two children at a time:

- Botanist: Cares for plants.

- Date Stamper: Stamps journal pages, sign-in books for centers, and anything else that needs to be dated.

- Attendance Taker: Records who's missing.

- Messenger: Transports messages to the main office or other classrooms.

- Mat Helper: Helps set out mats for the rest of the class.

- Pinch Hitter: Fills in for anyone who is sick and unable to do his job that day.

Jobs for up to four children at a time:

- Snack Helper: Assists in setting up for snack time.

Introduce jobs gradually, with a handful rather than the entire list, so children will have enough time to grasp fully what each one requires. When everyone is able to do a few jobs well, add more. Starting slowly will pay off, as children move toward functioning independently in many ways.

To help children identify their job assignments, create a pocket chart. Line pockets up in rows of three or four, allowing extra space at the bottom for adding jobs later in the school year. Under each pocket, write the job title. On each pocket, draw a representative picture. For example, for the electrician, you might draw a light bulb or wall switch. For the class comforter, you could draw two children hugging. Place name cards in the pockets to indicate who will carry out each job for the day or week. At the end of each day (or week), shift the name cards from left to right. That way, the children can anticipate their jobs.

Organizing the chart this way has another advantage: You give children an opportunity to "read" a chart, from left to right and then down to the left side of the next row, as if they were reading a book. This provides a good introduction to how print works on a page.

Introducing Class Pets

As children become comfortable in their new classroom, you might want to introduce class pets. Pets provide an opportunity to teach how to care for living things that are dependent on us. By creating safe environments for animals, children will be doing for the animals what you have done for them— making them feel at home in the classroom.

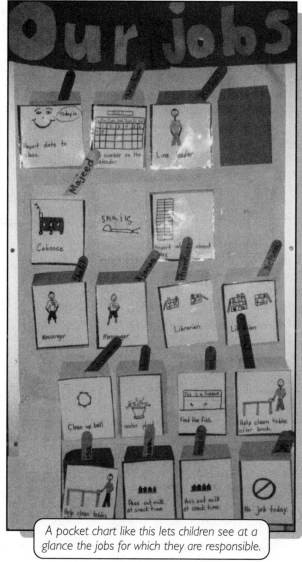
A pocket chart like this lets children see at a glance the jobs for which they are responsible.

What pet should you choose? You'd be surprised by the options. Guinea pigs, hamsters, and rabbits are common. But because they have fur and shed, you'll need to check to be sure that none of the children has allergies.

If you find that fur does make some of the children sneeze or scratch, consider land snails or fish. Snails can be ordered from most biological supply catalogs for about ten dollars a dozen. They eat all kinds of greens and can survive a week's vacation without new food or water.

Land snails are hearty and reproduce often. Babies grow quickly, giving children the opportunity to observe their development. They can be housed in a relatively small tank or terrarium. Children love watching snails as they crawl over the terrain, leaving their slime trail behind them. Your students will probably want to hold them, too. But until they learn the importance of being gentle, an adult should be with them when they remove animals from their home.

Goldfish and tropical fish require more maintenance than snails, but their bright colors and the gentle hum of the tank's filter make them appealing to many teachers. Parents who keep fish at home can provide advice as you and the children set up a classroom tank. Local pet-store owners may also be willing to share their knowledge. If possible, plan a field trip to a pet store to purchase the supplies you will need.

Making Special Books

During the first weeks of school, you can learn a great deal about your students, and they can find out about one another, by making "special books." These books require time and effort, but they're worth it. Follow these steps:

★ During the first week of school, send a letter home asking parents to send in up to six snapshots. Suggest pictures from a recent vacation or holidays at home, showing the child with loved ones or with a favorite pet or toy. Explain that the photos are for the child's special book, which will go home with him at the end of the school year.

★ If parents are unable to supply photographs, consider sending home a disposable camera or taking photographs of the child at school.

★ Paste the photos to card stock, one per page.

★ Sit with each child and ask her to tell you about the photograph. Write exactly what the child says underneath each photo.

★ Laminate front and back covers, or cover them with clear contact paper, and bind the book with metal rings.

★ When you have made a book for each child, read two a day to the class during morning meeting. As you read her book, invite the child to come to the front of the group. Let them respond to questions.

★ Place the books in the library area so the children can look at them on their own.

★ Throughout the year, add classroom photos of the children to their books.

By writing down what each child says about his photographs, you will learn a great deal about how he uses language. Does he speak in complete sentences? How extensive is his vocabulary? What kinds of expressions does he commonly use? You will also be communicating a powerful message to all the children: I want to know who you are, what you like, whom you love, and what you do outside of school.

As you read the books to the class, children will begin to make comparisons. "That's just like in Amy's book," someone may say. Or "I have a golden retriever, too!" Making these comparisons is natural, and it will foster deep discussions. As young children move into group settings, it's important to supply them with ways to hold onto what makes them unique, as well as what makes them resemble others. With special books, you can accomplish that.

It takes time for young children to "move in" to the classroom. In the first months, you should focus primarily on teaching children how to function independently and cooperate—basically, how to take care of themselves and one another. If you put this chapter's lessons at the heart of your curriculum, by mid-October or early November you will have gone a long way in accomplishing that. Children will internalize many of the rules and routines of the classroom. They will discover a great deal about one another by working and playing together. They will begin to take responsibility for the well being of others as they do their jobs each day. In sum, they will learn to be "at home" in their new classroom.

Chapter 3

Arrival Time

For young children who are making the transition from home to school, routines are critical. And having an arrival-time routine is particularly important in helping children adjust quickly to classroom life. (We use the term "arrival time" to mean the twenty minutes or so between a child's entrance and the start of the morning meeting.) It's easy to create such a routine. By posting a chart that clearly spells out routines and reinforcing those routines through dialogue, you can communicate what children should do when they arrive:

★ Put things like coats and backpacks away.

★ "Sign in" on the attendance chart.

★ Say hello to your friends.

★ Do your job, if it is one that can be done during this time.

Sharing Accomplishments With Parents

If, after the first weeks of school, you allow adults to accompany children into the classroom, arrival time gives children a chance to share their work. A block building that a child has been working on for days, an entry in a writing journal, a new painting that demonstrates emerging artistic skills—these are all accomplishments a young child may be eager to talk about.

Some teachers use the time to speak with parents. During a short morning chat, you can alert them to upcoming school activities, or direct them to examples of their children's work that demonstrate growth.

This visit also gives parents the chance to tell you about important things that might be happening in the family. You may discover that a baby is on the way, that one parent has a new job that requires travel, or

Post a chart to reinforce arrival-time routines.

simply that a child didn't get much sleep the previous night. Your openness may even make them comfortable enough to raise more serious concerns. If that happens, schedule an appointment to talk more fully, in private.

During arrival time, you might also encourage children and their parents to:
- Read a favorite story together
- Review the morning schedule
- Visit the pets
- Admire work the children have done in the centers

No matter how the time is spent, those first twenty minutes provide good opportunities for children to share their brave new world—the classroom—with those they love most. It also gives parents a chance to get a glimpse of what's happening at school.

Gathering News of the Day

At the start of each day, Lenore Furman, jots down her students' news in a notebook.

Collecting children's "news of the day" is another effective arrival time activity, one that supports their emerging literacy. Position yourself in a special spot. As children enter, ask if they would like to share some news from home. Write down exactly what they say in a composition book. Each child will watch enthusiastically as his words are transformed from sound into print.

Be sure to include the child's name with each entry. As children learn to recognize their names, as well as the names of their friends, they will begin to look for them in the news-of-the-day book. Putting boxes around names makes it easier to locate them.

Monday, Nov. 15

[Rebecca] Last night I went to Nickolia's house. We watched the Lion King and ate pizza. It was fun.
[Jose] My tooth came out!
[Marcus] My Mom went to California. I miss her.

A page from a "News of the Day" notebook.

By asking children for their news, you give them a chance to talk about what's happening in their lives outside the classroom. It's another way to strengthen the bridge between home and school. Children will talk about all kinds of things such as a shopping trip, a movie, even what they had for dinner. They might also bring up difficult subjects such as the death of a grandparent, a fire in their neighborhood, or something that scared them. Ask each child if you may share her news with the whole group. If a child has experienced a particularly painful event, she may resist. It's important to respect her wishes.

Typically, you'll collect enough items to read at morning meeting. But if children have many things to report, you may need extra time to write up the news, perhaps while the children are working in the writing center. Then you can read it just before dismissal.

Giving children the opportunity to bring the "stuff" of their lives into the classroom requires courage. You must be willing to talk with them about whatever they tell you. The simple act of asking for and recording their news tells them that you're interested in their lives outside of school and that they can talk to you about anything. These one-to-one exchanges build trust. And when children hear each other's news, and talk about it, they learn more about themselves and others.

Other Arrival-Time Activities

Between the time parents leave and morning meeting begins, children should be able to choose from a limited number of free-choice activities that require little clean-up. News of the day is one. Others include:

★ Working with play dough

★ Drawing and writing

★ Looking at books in the library area

★ Building with math manipulatives at a table

Letting children know that it's time to switch gears can be a big challenge. So when it's time for morning meeting, try using a visual or sound cue such as flashing the overhead lights, ringing a bell, or playing a short tune on a xylophone. It's best to use one signal consistently, so the children will grow to recognize and respond to it promptly. Explain that the correct response to this signal is to clean up and quietly move to the meeting area.

Chapter 4

Morning Meeting

Helping children function well in a group should be a vital part of any early childhood curriculum. Morning meeting—the time when the class gathers together on the rug to discuss the day, its schedule, and other issues—provides just the right setting for such lessons. It's the perfect context for teaching children how to behave confidently and fairly in a group, and how to take turns talking and listening to each other.

To ensure a successful morning meeting, start by thinking through the physical arrangement of your meeting area. Children should be able to see you, their classmates, and the daily schedule and chart. Therefore, positioning them in a semicircle, rather than in rows, is preferable. You should sit near the schedule and chart, in a low chair, so you can point to them as you and the children read.

Meeting Manners

Just as children are taught table manners, they need to be taught meeting manners. This may not be as easy as it sounds, especially when it comes to talking in turns and listening to one another. Before day one, you must decide if you are going to let children speak freely or ask them to raise their hands and wait until they're called on before they speak. Requiring them to raise their hands enables you to keep the group focused while giving many children a chance to speak. But you will always be the gatekeeper for the conversation. Don't be surprised if some children start directing their remarks to you rather than to one another. However, if you allow children to present ideas without waiting for you to call on them, the conversation could get out of control.

Your decision might depend on your children's prior experiences in group settings. Kindergarteners, for example, may be able to converse with little gatekeeping on your part because of meeting manners they learned in preschool. Very often, these children arrive knowing how to listen to one another and how to process what is being said. You may have to intervene occasionally with questions such as, "Can anyone tell me what they heard Marcus saying about his trip to the museum?" or "Christine, do you agree with what Elizabeth said? Why?" That way, you act more as facilitator. Your interventions will help children develop the skills to think about what their classmates say and whether they agree. These are skills most kindergarteners can master, given time and attention from you.

Another way to encourage child-to-child conversation, without playing gatekeeper, is to let children call on one another. For example, if a child brings something to share with the group, have him ask others to raise their hands if they have questions. Then let him call on his classmates, one by one. Similarly, if you have created special books and read them at morning meeting, the child featured in the book can field comments or questions about it. (See Chapter 2, page 26, for instructions on making special books.)

Keeping meetings brief, twenty to thirty minutes, and focusing on topics that children care about, minimizes disruptions, too. Of course, it takes only one child to create a stir. Every teacher has had a child who can't sit still, won't listen to others, and continues talking when it's not her turn. Address the situation by first asking the child to sit next to you, where you can keep a friendly hand on her knee or whisper a gentle reminder that it's time to pay attention. If that doesn't work, try positioning the child in a chair at the edge of the group so that her distractions are not central.

In the end, though, you might have to accept the fact that some young children are not ready to participate in a group. If that's the case, have an assistant teacher or an adult volunteer sit with the child in an area of the room where she can concentrate on a quiet task, without bothering others. Explain it to the group this way: "Kevin isn't going to be in the group today. He needs to have his own space. When he's ready to join us, he will." This signals to the rest of the class that Kevin is fine and his situation is temporary.

Meeting Agenda

What do you talk about during morning meeting? Structuring the discussion around children's interests and your expectations is a good rule of thumb.

News of the Day

Reading the news of the day, which you can collect from students at arrival time, is a good way to begin. (See Chapter 3, page 30, for more information on news of the day.) As children hear their news read, they feel special and empowered. Their news can stimulate a host of conversations about upcoming vacations, new pets, weekend visits from grandparents, and more. Again, make sure these exchanges occur among the children as well as between you and the child.

Daily Schedule

After discussing events that occurred outside school, move on to events that will happen in school by reviewing the daily schedule. At the beginning of the year, you may want to announce and post events, card by card. (See Chapter 2, page 23 for instructions on creating schedule cards.) Say something like, "Today we will have our meeting. After meeting is work time. Then we'll have a snack . . . ." After a few weeks of reviewing the schedule this way, you can post all the cards before the children arrive.

Ask volunteers to read the cards as you point to them. Once the children can recognize the words, ask questions like, "What comes before music? What is the last thing we will do today? After recess, where do we go?" This is a good way to foster a greater understanding of terms such as "before," "after," "next," "last," and "first."

Morning Message ☼

After you've covered the day's schedule, direct the children's attention to the morning message, which is best presented on a chart of oversized lined paper. For pre-K children, use colored markers and picture cues to help them make sense of the words. Write the message either before school or during the morning arrival time. Here's what it might look like:

Hello boys and girls. (written in green)

Today is Tuesday. (in blue)

Andre, Samantha, and Zachary will go on a trip outside school today. (in purple, with a picture of three children walking)

Amanda, Marcus, and Eli will cook today. (in red, with a picture of a measuring cup)

Today is Jillian's birthday! (in orange, with a picture of a cupcake and candle)

We will finish making our mural of the park today. (in black)

A simple, consistent message is most understandable. If you always begin with a "hello" sentence written in the same color, children will quickly learn how to read it, even though they may not yet know the names of the letters in the sentence, or the difference even between letters and words. Just as children learn to read the word "McDonald's" because of the golden arches or "Stop" because of the red sign on the street corner, children will learn to read a consistent opening sentence.

Children love knowing when it's their turn to do something special, so many of them will scan the message quickly for their names. As children gain familiarity with names, they will begin to read other parts of the sentences as well. If you always use red for the sentence that tells who will cook, along with a picture of a measuring cup, they will gradually begin to read that sentence. Similarly, by using consistent color and picture cues for other sentences that appear regularly, children will be able to figure out who is doing

Consistent use of language and color helps students read the message.

what on any given day. Ask, "Who wants to read the cooking sentence?" and see how many children volunteer. They may need help decoding names, but other children will surely provide assistance. Encourage that behavior. It demonstrates that everyone, not just you, can be counted on for assistance.

Reading and confidence go hand in hand, so always make sure children feel secure when they read aloud. Remember never to ask a child to read aloud a sentence that contains unfamiliar words. Instead, read those sentences first, pointing to each word as you go.

A morning message for kindergarteners should be slightly more sophisticated than the one described above for preschool children. Here's an example:

Good morning wonderful students.
Today we will finish our interview questions for the security guard.
Rosa's mother is coming in to cook with us today. We will make homemade tortillas.
If it stops raining, we will go outside today.
Have a great day!
Ms. Sneed

Since kindergarteners are generally more aware of sound-symbol relationships, you may want to write out the message during meeting time. Tell the children each word as you write it, and then ask them to listen for the sounds. Can they match those letters and sounds? As they help you determine which letters you need, you will be modeling how they should be listening for sounds in words when they're writing on their own. For more on this topic, read *Getting the Most Out of Morning Message and Other Shared Writing Lessons* by Carleen daCruz Payne and Mary Browning Schulman (Scholastic Teaching Resources, 1998).

Weather Calendar

In many early childhood classrooms, teachers devote much of morning meeting to discussing dates, days of the week, and months of the year, but these concepts can be very abstract to many young children. Instead, you may want to use a calendar to record the weather. Make your calendar from a piece of eighteen-by-twenty-four-inch painting paper. Be sure date blocks are large enough for children to draw pictures that represent each day's weather.

Kindergarten children often draw suns, clouds, raindrops, and snowmen. If a child's drawing doesn't capture the weather clearly, ask her for a word that describes it and write it below her picture.

Have the children use tally marks to keep track of the number of sunny, cloudy, raining, windy, and snowy days in each month. At the end of the month, count the tallies and create a bar graph that illustrates weather patterns. If you do this routinely, the children can compare bar graphs from month to month to find out which month had the most rainy days, sunny days, snowy days, and so on.

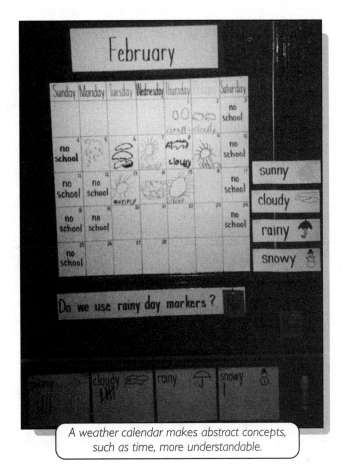

A weather calendar makes abstract concepts, such as time, more understandable.

By "counting the days" this way, children will not only begin to learn about months, days, and dates, but they will also find themselves engaged in activities centered on something meaningful to them—the weather, which often determines whether they'll spend play time inside or out.

Class Jobs

In the beginning of the school year, you should spend part of meeting time reviewing the job chart. (See Chapter 2, page 23, for more information on assigning jobs.) Ask each child to read the chart and tell the group what job he has for that week and at what point in the day he plans to carry it out. Discussing jobs during meeting allows you to remind children of their responsibilities and to explain what particular tasks entail.

New Materials ☀

At morning meeting, you might also discuss new materials you've brought into the classroom. For example, if you're introducing as measuring cups, show the cups, explain what they are, and ask the children where they should be stored. Some children may want them in the sand/water table. Others might suggest the cooking center. When all suggestions are in, have the children vote. Explain that the suggestion that gets the most votes wins. Later, as a class, you can decide if the measuring cups should be moved.

Asking where materials belong teaches children how to categorize. And voting on the best spot, and the length of time the materials will remain in that spot, fosters problem-solving skills. For example, the group might decide that two measuring cups should be stored at the sand/water table and two at the cooking center.

Preparation for Center Work ☀

Preparing students for work time is a good use of meeting time, too. You might want to demonstrate how a new material such as clay is used. Show the children how the clay is worked by pinching it, poking holes in it with a finger, rolling it between your palms, and flattening it with the heel of your hand. You can also explain clean-up procedures. Later in the day, when the children go to the art center, they'll be ready.

Morning meeting can also be used to advise children on ways to extend activities at different centers. If the children have been playing house in the dramatic play area, for instance, ask the group for other ideas. One child might propose playing supermarket. Another, bringing a sick pet to the vet. Let the group vote and proclaim the result, "Today, if you want to go to the dramatic-play center, it will be a vet's office."

You could also initiate a broader discussion of a topic you intend to study. For example, if you are beginning a unit on the neighborhood, you might ask, "What's in your neighborhood?" This will build children's background knowledge by prompting a conversation about merchants, services, parks, and other features of the community.

After twenty to thirty minutes of sitting, most children are eager to get up and move. Sending them off to work in centers shouldn't be difficult. At the beginning of the year, it's important to reserve the end of morning meeting for reviewing choices children have for work time and helping them make their selections. As the school year progresses, children will become more independent about figuring out where they can go. Regardless of the time of year, though, center options must be clear in order for the children to make informed choices.

Chapter 5

Off to Work: Centers

It's 10:30 A.M. in Lenore Furman's kindergarten class, and all her students are happily going off to work at the various centers located around her classroom. Centers are designated areas for particular kinds of activities. Ms. Furman's classroom features these centers:

- ★ Table Toys
- ★ Drawing and Writing
- ★ Art
- ★ Blocks
- ★ Science and Math
- ★ Library
- ★ Dramatic Play

Each center is self-contained and stocked with the necessary materials. As the children work, Ms. Furman moves about the classroom so that she can observe, record, and assist. Her students know she is available to help if they get "stuck" or can't resolve a conflict. They also know that she will comment on their progress as she watches them, validating and supporting their efforts.

The Benefits of Centers

Centers require much more effort than whole-group activities. But whole-group activities do not give children the opportunities to make choices and work collaboratively. Without such opportunities, children's voices are only infrequently heard, making a community where everyone's ideas and interests matter impossible.

By working in centers, children learn to work independently and cooperatively, and to make choices about their work. As a result, they feel more at home in the classroom because they have some control over what they do. Centers are definitely worth your time and effort.

Teacher Tip

"Float" to Facilitate Children's Work

Floating during work time enables you to be available to all and anyone who needs you. It leaves you free to encourage a large number of children at once, and assess their work. Simple comments such as, "You thought you couldn't, but you did!" and "Wow, that's the biggest design you've ever made! Where did you begin?" create work times that are calm, productive, and organized. They also demonstrate that you're paying attention to the children, discovering what they can do, what they are struggling with—that you're finding those "teachable moments" to help them move towards the next level of understanding.

Starting Up Centers

At the beginning of the year, children need help learning how to use materials, where to store them, and how to clean up. Use the morning meeting to teach these lessons. It's best to introduce a few centers at a time, but provide enough of them so that everyone has a place to work. Ideally, there should be room for four or five children at each center. This number could vary, though, depending on the size of your class and classroom.

Limit the number of materials at each center, too, in the beginning. For example, only plain paper, crayons, and colored pencils in the Drawing and Writing Center, and only play dough in the art center. Not only will this make centers easier to manage, it will promote sharing and talking among children because they'll be

working with similar materials. Just be sure to provide enough of those materials for everyone.

As children grow comfortable working independently, introduce more centers and materials. Part of feeling at home in the classroom is knowing where things are and how to put them back. Keeping centers simple in the beginning will go a long way in establishing that feeling quickly.

Create Your Own Dough

Making your own play dough is easy. This recipe serves up enough for up to five children. As the year progresses, and if you have access to cooking facilities, consider making it together with your students.

Cooked Play Dough

2 cups flour	2 tablespoons oil	4 teaspoons crème of tarter
1 cup salt	2 cups water	a few drops of food coloring

Combine and cook ingredients in a pot or frying pan, on medium heat. Stir until the mixture congeals. Once it cools, knead it and store it in an airtight container. The dough will last a couple of months if you keep it sealed and unrefrigerated when not in use. If you double the recipe, stirring the mixture as it cooks is difficult. Therefore, it's better to make additional small batches.

Tools for Choosing Centers

Work time usually lasts from 45 minutes to an hour in most preschools and kindergartens. During this time, children learn a lot more than the task at hand. They learn to make choices, work alone and in groups, respect that there's room for only a certain number of children at each center, and, eventually, to move from center to center independently.

Younger children will need extra guidance. Helping them choose centers wisely should be your first mission. These three tools should come in handy: "Picture Your Work" Choice Chart; Clothespin Choice Board; and "Children at Work" Road Signs.

"Picture Your Work" Choice Chart ☼

Using a chart during morning meeting is probably the simplest way to help children choose and to keep track of their choices. On a large piece of paper, draw simple pictures to represent each center, ask children to make a selection, and write their names below the picture. As you list their names, send them off individually to their chosen center.

The pictures enable children to "read" the chart. The numbers make clear how many children can work in a given center. The names provide you with a record of children's choices. Keep the chart posted in the meeting area for reference. You may want to use this system all year or replace it with one of the other methods.

Clothespin Choice Board ☼

Once children are familiar with all the centers, you can introduce this system, which allows greater independence. On different colored pieces of construction paper, write the centers' names and mount or draw pictures that represent them. Paint clothespins to match each color and attach them to the pictures. By color coding the board this way, children will be able to use it on their own, even if they can't read the name of the center. Once a child has chosen his center, he removes the clothespin and attaches it to his clothing as a reminder of where he's supposed to be working.

The number of clothespins per picture is determined by the maximum number of children per center. If, for example, you decide there is only room for four children

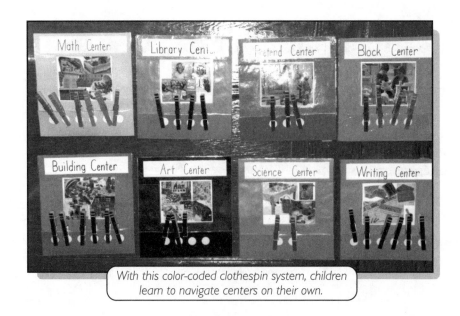

With this color-coded clothespin system, children learn to navigate centers on their own.

in the block center, then you would attach only four clothespins to the corresponding Choice Board picture. If all four clothespins for the block center are missing, it will be obvious to children that that center is "full" and they need to make a different choice.

This system also allows children to shift centers during work time. They can return to the meeting area, replace the clothespin for their first choice, and choose another one. And they can do this all by themselves and without having to check every center to see if there's room.

"Children at Work" Road Signs ☼

Another alternative, which is especially good for older children, is a series of "Children at Work" signs that resemble "men at work" signs commonly found at construction sites. Create one sign for each center with stick figures representing the maximum number of children who can work there.

At morning meeting, ask who would like to work where, sending no more than the maximum number of children to each center. If a child wants to join a different center during work time, it's easy for him to determine if there's room: He compares the center's maximum number (as indicated on the sign) to the number of his classmates who are actually working there. While this system doesn't give teachers a record of children's choices, it does give students a great deal of counting practice.

Tools for Keeping Track of Choices

It's important to have a formal method for keeping track of children's choices, so you can see where they like to work, with whom they like to work, and in what direction they might need gentle nudging.

Center Choices Checklist ☼

With the center choices checklist, you can assemble data over a few weeks. (See Appendix.) From there, create a chart like the one on the next page to get a sense of how the children are spending their time. Note: dates along the top are listed twice to indicate morning and afternoon.

Name/Date	13	13	14	14	15	15	16	16	17	17	20	20	21	21	22	22	23	23	24	24
Center Choices Chart, September 13–September 24:																				
Elizabeth	B	A	M	W	Sc	Sa	D	T	W	B	W	D	A	T	Sa	B	B	D	L	Sc
John	B	B	B	L	B	T	W	A	B	T	M	B	Sc	L	A	B	D	M	B	
Maria	T	T	M	D	D	D	T	M	M	W	W	W	W	L	L	W	M	M	M	W

Code for each center, B = blocks, A = art, M = math, W = writing, Sc = science, Sa = sand, D = dramatic play, T = table toys, L = library

Observational Notes ☼

To note the work a child has done in a particular center or an exchange she has had with another child, carry a clipboard containing a sheet that lists each center, with room for you to jot down observations.

Instead of a clipboard, you can use stick-on notes to record data, which you can put into a file box and sort out later in the day, when you have time.

Sign-In Books ☼

Once children can write their own names, place sign-in books at every center. Date each page for the day and ask children to jot down their names before beginning work. This, too, will give you a record of their work-time choices.

Checklists, notes, and sign-in books may also prove useful in helping you resolve complaints, such as, "Tommy goes to blocks all the time. I never get a chance." By looking together at a record, you and the child can determine when she was last in the block center and if, in fact, Tommy has had more time there than she has.

A page from Kathleen Hayes's observational notes.

A Close-Up Look at Specific Kinds of Centers

Establishing centers requires good organization and management to ensure that children are engaging in developmentally appropriate experiences. Think carefully about the materials you put in your centers, as well as the work that goes on in them. Consider also how you will assess and extend that work. Here are some things to think about for specific kinds of centers, those most common to pre-kindergarten and kindergarten classrooms.

Table Toys Center

Possible Materials:

* Legos and/or Duplos
* Colored wooden beads
* Table blocks
* Puzzles
* String
* Bristle blocks
* Peg boards

How to Store Materials:

Use see-through bins. On labels, write the name of the materials and draw simple pictures to assist children who may not be able to read the names. Store the bins on shelves with identical labels so that children can easily return toys to their proper spot.

Sign-in books are a great way to track children's center choices over time.

Remember, at the beginning of the year, it's best to place only a few different kinds of materials in each center. If, for example, you have a large quantity of one kind of manipulative, share it with several children. The children will be more likely to cooperate and learn from one another, since they'll be working with the same materials.

Using table toys develops fine motor skills since children must use both their hands and their minds to build things. Some children may become so engrossed in a project that it takes them days to complete it. Make sure you're ready for such works in progress by reserving a "saving shelf," where children can store their unfinished projects for a subsequent work period. It's also a good holding spot for work they might want to talk about in a share meeting. For example, at the end of a recent work time, Ms. Furman invited the children to join her on the rug. She asked if anyone wanted to share something.

Jeremy said, "Michael and I worked on our zoo in the block area. We made five areas for the animals, and the one for the bears had a real high wall."

"I know you've worked on that for a couple of days. Are you done now or will you need more time tomorrow in blocks?" Ms. Furman responded.

Jeremy and Michael both agreed they thought they would need more time. Ms. Furman then asked if they needed more helpers in the block area. They said, "Sure."

When children share their work with the whole group this way, they quickly become the experts. When someone wants help at a later date, making a Lego car perhaps, he will know to go to Rebecca, who once made just such a car during work time and shared it with the group. By recognizing one another as teachers, children come to view the classroom as a true learning community.

Drawing and Writing Center

Possible Materials:

- ★ Beginner black pencils
- ★ Crayons
- ★ Folded paper for making blank books
- ★ Children's scissors
- ★ Chalk boards and chalk
- ★ Individual drawing and writing books

- ★ Beginner colored pencils
- ★ Plain paper
- ★ Cut-up chart paper
- ★ Dry-erase boards and markers
- ★ A file for each child
- ★ Date stamp

How to Store Materials:

Use coffee cans or small baskets for pencils and crayons. Label shelves with pictures and words to show where the containers belong. Store an assortment of paper on shelves or in stackable trays.

Well-organized drawing and writing supplies

Most children love to draw and write. And they usually do so sitting around a table, happily conversing with friends, while working on their latest manuscript, letter, or illustration. Having a wealth of supplies, like those listed on the previous page, enables children to try new things, master different effects, and avoid conflicts since there is enough for everyone.

To heighten community at the drawing and writing center, find ways to encourage children to share their work. These three supplies are a must: a class picture dictionary, a class mailbox, and a cutting bucket.

Picture Dictionary

To help children learn the names and faces of their classmates, create a "first dictionary" from their photos. A simple album is all you need. Keep it in the drawing and writing center so children can refer to it when composing a letter, creating a drawing, or scribbling a note to a friend.

Teacher Tip

Dried-Up Markers? Try Pencils Instead

Colored pencils, particularly the fat ones with extra-soft lead, are much less expensive, last longer, and provide better line definition than markers. And, best of all, children love them. For special occasions and rainy days, keep a set of markers available as a treat.

"My Own" Mailbox

Individual mailboxes prompt children to send drawings and notes to one another. You can make them from half-gallon milk cartons. Cut off their tops and let children decorate them with colored paper, stickers, or adhesive/contact paper. Put each child's name on a mailbox, then glue the boxes together, side by side.

An over-the-door shoe caddy makes a great mail center.

The Cutting Bucket

If you write your morning message on chart paper, think about creating a "Cutting Bucket." At the end of each day, cut or tear sentences from the morning message and place them in a dishpan or small bucket. When children want to add familiar text to their work, they'll have a ready supply. With a piece of scotch tape, they can also make nametags for themselves and friends.

Make Class Get-Well Cards

If the classroom is to be a place where children feel at home, then they need to know they are missed when they're out sick. Keep pieces of folded card stock in the writing area for children to create cards to send friends who are ill. Have children place their cards in the absent child's mailbox. Once the mailbox is full, gather the cards and send them home in a large envelope that you and the children address together.

Tools for Keeping Track

One of the easiest and most efficient ways to keep track of students' work is with individual Drawing and Writing Books, which can be stored in the center. Use two sheets of 9-by-12-inch construction paper or card stock for the covers, and about twenty sheets of plain white paper for the interior pages. Staple down the left-hand side to bind the books and write the children's names on the front.

For older children who have begun to write letters and words, you may want to include pages with lines at the bottom to encourage some writing. (See Appendix.) You can do this by using preprinted primary story paper or photocopying plain paper with one or two hand-drawn lines.

Teacher Tip

Use Colored Book Covers to Save Time and Build Independence

By offering a variety of colors for covers, you'll make it easier for children to find their books. For example, if Elizabeth can't read her own name yet, but knows that her book is red and her name begins with E, then she doesn't have to waste as much time identifying which book is hers.

When you introduce the books to the group, explain that they are for drawings and writings that the children may want to keep at school. For work children may want to take home, it's better to use loose, single sheets of paper. Also, encourage children to date each page they create, using a date stamp. That way, when you and parents

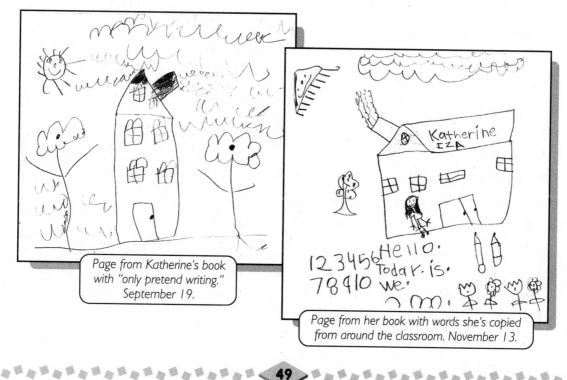

Page from Katherine's book with "only pretend writing." September 19.

Page from her book with words she's copied from around the classroom. November 13.

look through the children's books at conference time, you'll get a better sense of how their work is changing and developing over time.

Art Center

Possible Materials:

★ **For Painting:**

Tempera paint

Water containers and sponges

Trays for holding paint supplies

Small lids or furniture coasters

Jumbo watercolor sets

★ **For Collage:**

A variety of papers and fabrics

Glue in small containers

Small and large pieces of cardboard

Divided boxes for storing materials

Glue brushes

★ **For Drawing:**

Black pencils

Soft ebony pencils

Paper

Colored pencils

Crayons

★ **For Clay:**

Standard gray clay

Clay boards

★ **Play Dough:**

Cookie cutters and rollers

Place mats for rolling dough

★ **For Constructions:**

Small boxes

Small plastic bottles

Small pieces of wood

Empty film canisters

Jar lids

Colored pipe cleaners

Corks

How to Store Materials:

★ Paint Supplies: a shelf children can reach easily

★ Construction Supplies: a cart with stacked bins

★ Pencils and Crayons: cans covered with contact paper

★ White Glue: baby food jars with loose-fitting lids

★ Glue Brushes, Paint Sponges, Lids used for painting, and Cookie Cutters: plastic quart containers

★ Play Dough: airtight container

★ Clay: covered bucket

All materials should be stored on shelves labeled with a picture and the name of materials so children know where to return them.

Young children enjoy drawing, painting, sculpting, and making collages and constructions. By using open-ended materials like the ones suggested on the previous page, they discover the power of imagination.

Start the year with the easiest-to-use materials, and then gradually add more complex ones. Introduce new materials or project ideas to the whole group during morning meeting. Then let children explore on their own at the art center.

Creating Gallery Space ☼

Finding room to display children's art is not always easy, but it's necessary since it sends out a strong message that their work is worthy of being viewed and admired. Turning a particular classroom wall into your art gallery may solve the problem. Hallway walls, bulletin boards, and even bathroom walls may also be available. Consider assigning a spot to each child, labeled with her name, and use it for her artwork all year round. Each time a child produces a new

Children creating a mural in the art center

work, ask if she would like to replace what's currently hanging in her spot with the latest piece. This gives you an opportunity to talk to each child about her work and to let her know how much you value what she's done. Additionally, as new work goes on the wall, children gather ideas from one another about possible ways to work.

Tools for Keeping Track

As children produce art throughout the year, storing it for parent meetings and evaluation purposes becomes difficult. Constructions are often large and must be sent home shortly after they are made. Similarly, collages may be hard to store when children have used three-dimensional objects such as buttons, corks, and small pieces of wood.

Paintings are a little less problematic; they can be stored in files, on racks, and in wooden boxes with dividers. But if none of these solutions is available, create "pizza box portfolios." Go to local pizzerias and ask owners to donate or sell at cost new pizza boxes.

Label each box with a child's name, and keep paintings, collages, and other flat work in it. You may want to form boxes inside out, so that advertising messages don't show. That way, children can decorate and personalize the outside.

Once they become comfortable deciding what to put into their portfolios, what hangs in the gallery, and what they want to take home, children will come to trust their own judgment. They will be more likely to say, "I like this because—" rather than seeking approval from adults.

Block Center ☼

Possible Materials:

★ **Unit Blocks**

★ **Accessories:**
Small cars and trucks   Small people and animal figures

★ **Labeling Supplies:**
Scraps of construction paper   Pencils
Tape

★ **References:**
Books   Photographs

How to Store Materials:

Label shelves with colored contact paper to help children determine where different kinds of blocks belong. People, animals, and writing supplies can be stored in plastic bins. Books can be displayed on shelf tops. Post photographs of interesting buildings on nearby walls, at children's eye level.

For safety reasons, introducing materials slowly is particularly important in the block area. As children learn how to use small blocks properly, and restore them to their rightful storage spaces, provide larger ones and more accessories. At the start of the year, a few figures and a large toy truck or two should be enough. Once children learn the routines in the block area, and have begun to explore what they can do as a group, extend their activities and help them work together to build a strong sense of community.

Cut block shapes from contact paper and affix them to shelves to facilitate clean-up.

Building Shared Spaces and Places

Children often decide to work individually, creating structures that reflect spaces and places they know. Sometimes, however, you may want to provide a common focus in the block area that will prompt children to work together and find connections among their constructions. Here are a few examples:

The Reference Book

After discussing various features of their block buildings, Kathleen Hayes took her pre-K class at the Bank Street School for Children to visit and photograph interesting details on the buildings of Columbia University, which is a short walk from the school. Each child was allowed to take two photographs. All the children searched

long and hard before deciding on their two shots. One child photographed the pattern in a brick sidewalk. Another chose a front door surrounded by columns and topped with a triangular shape. Kathleen kept careful notes about what the children shot and created a book containing the photographs and simple captions such as "Jeremy's photograph of Columbia" and "Sarah's photograph of Columbia." This book was kept in the block area for children to use as a reference while working there. Because of this field trip and reference book, the children's block work became more elaborate.

The Church

Three children in Ms. Furman's kindergarten classroom decided to build a church similar to the one that their classmate Bobby attends. First, they built a tall tower. Bobby arranged blocks on the top of the tower in the shape of a cross. Then all the children worked on the church's walls. They created pews from small rectangular blocks and doors that swung open. When they were ready to build the roof, one child asked, "Where are all the people?"

Ms. Furman had not yet put any figure accessories in her block area. As her students became proficient builders, erecting structures they wanted to use for dramatic play, they all became hungry for props. Ms. Furman gathered the children on the rug to discuss how they could make people for their block buildings. Having had some experience in the art center creating large-scale people and animals from cardboard, the class decided to make smaller ones. They used lightweight cardboard for bodies, decorating them with wallpaper samples and bits of yarn and fabric. To help the figures stand up, they inserted them into Plasticine bases. When the figures got "injured" (i.e., bent or torn) the children transferred them to a cardboard box that had been transformed into a "hospital."

The River

A group of four-year-olds in Kathleen Hayes's class were interested in boats. In the math and science center, they made simple boats from paper, wood, and Styrofoam to use at their water table. Ms. Hayes then talked with them about building boats and bridges in the block center. She and the children used watered-down blue tempera to paint a wide river on the floor, which influenced the children to make a variety of "seaworthy vessels" to go into the river, bridges to go over it, and buildings for its banks.

The Street

Newark, New Jersey, teacher Dina Rios took her kindergarten class on a walk outside, down the school's block. On clipboards, the children drew what they saw along the way. When they returned to the classroom, Ms. Rios used watered-down yellow and black tempera paint to depict a road on the block area's floor and encouraged her students to build what they had seen on the street. Besides buildings, the children decided they wanted to make cars. After discussing how they might do that, a handful of them went to the art center, which contained recycled materials the children had collected from home. Using small boxes, glue, and water-bottle lids, and armed with persistence, the children made their own cars. Some even took string and connected several cars to make a train.

Tools for Keeping Track

Photograph the children's block buildings and get a double set of prints made. One print can go in the child's portfolio, and the other can be inserted into a class book featuring the collected work of your young architects. Affix each photo to a piece of card stock, write what the child tells you about his building under the photo, punch holes along each page's edge, and use metal rings to bind the book. Invite the children to come up with a title such as Our Book of Building Blocks. Photos can be added throughout the year.

Science and Math Center

Possible Materials:

★ For the Sand Table:
Smooth stones or shells	Small plastic trucks
Shovels and buckets	Funnels
Sieves	Small cups
Plastic measuring cups	

★ For the Water Table:
Small plastic boats	Plastic measuring cups
Funnels	Plastic tubing with connectors
Corks	Water wheels
Bubbles	Food coloring

★ For Math Activities:
Jumbo Cusinaire rods	Pattern blocks
Unifix cubes	Geoboards

Dice   Playing cards

Puzzles

Simple board games that promote math skills such as counting, matching, and sequencing

★ **For Science Activities:**

Classroom pets and plants

How to Store Materials:

★ Math Manipulatives: clear plastic bins with matching labels on the bin and the shelf on which it's stored

★ Water and Sand Toys: small dishpans, clearly labeled with a picture of the object

★ Pets and Plants: a tank on a table or shelf at children's eye level, enabling them to care for the pets and plants. Placing living things at eye level will also facilitate children's observations.

Math Manipulatives

Young children need time to make their own discoveries about mathematical concepts. Therefore, what you provide should allow for open-ended exploration and play. Building with jumbo Cusinaire rods or creating their own designs with pattern blocks, for example, are good places to start.

When you begin doing math with the children in small groups, you can introduce complex games and tasks, as well as the materials that accompany them. Once children are comfortable carrying out games and tasks, you can move materials to the math and science center permanently. For example, if you introduce "Racing Dice" during a small-group time, store the dice and worksheets in the math and science center for children to use independently during work time. (See Chapter 6 for details.)

Teacher Tip

Bring the Natural World Indoors

When children go to school in the fall, many of them have spent time by the shore, so they may be familiar with natural objects that come from there. Collect small stones and shells from your trips to the beach and "hide" them in the sand table. Children can use sieves and other sand tools to find them. And, when they do, they'll be delighted.

Water and Sand Tables ☼

Water and sand are familiar, inviting materials. As children play with them, they will discover what happens to water when it runs through a wheel or a plastic tube. Let them scoop and fill bottles with sand or water, and find out facts on their own—for example, even though two bottles are shaped differently, they may hold the same amount of water.

Children working at the sand tables

Pets ☼

Imani, Justin, and Rachel are gathered around the science table. Rachel has taken an adult snail out of the tank and placed it carefully in the palm of her hand. She watches in amazement as the legs come out, followed by the head and foot. "Ooooh," she said as the snail begins crawling up her arm. "It tickles."

Many early childhood and primary classrooms have pets—and for good reason. By caring for them, children learn important lessons in responsibility. By observing and recording changes over time, they also learn about how animals thrive. If you're concerned about allergies to furry animals, though, consider raising snails.

Land snails, like turtles, come out of their shells only when they feel safe. Children love to hold them and watch them slowly emerge. If you have land snails in your part of the world, collect them and bring them into the classroom. If you don't, order them from biological supply companies. A few inches of water-sprayed, potting soil at the bottom of a small tank and a mesh lid is all you need to create a sustainable environment for the snails.

Children can try different types of food to see what snails prefer. And, since snails reproduce quickly, they can watch throughout the year as babies grow and develop into mature snails.

Tools for Keeping Track

Journals and graphs are important tools for recording observations, conducting experiments, and making sense of data.

Journals enable children to note changes they notice in class pets or plants. They also give you an opportunity to monitor children's awareness and understanding of simple concepts. For example, young children may be able to record in pictures, numbers, or words what foods their snails eat, how many adult snails they see, or how many buds are on the class geranium.

Graphs that children create as they explore math manipulatives also provide you

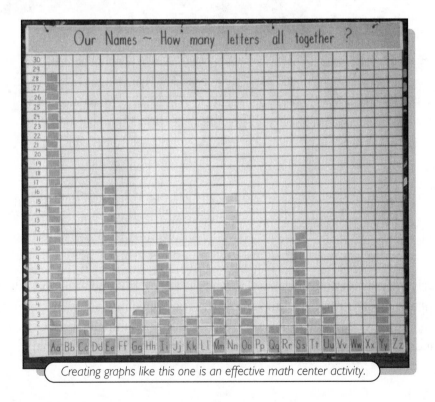

Creating graphs like this one is an effective math center activity.

with valuable information. Using simple graph forms, children can record the answers to such questions as, "How many different shaped pattern blocks can you pick up in one hand?" and "How many Unifix cubes does it take to measure the bookcase?" You can then analyze the results together.

Library Center

Possible Materials:

- Books
- Headphones
- Soft pillows
- Large cardboard box to serve as a nook
- Tape recorder
- Tapes
- Overstuffed chair or sofa

How to Store Materials:

Children need to be able to find the book they want. If you have many books, organize them by subject and store them in labeled bins or labeled areas on shelves. To help children return books correctly, label the bins and the books that go with them with identical stickers. Books-and-tape sets can be stored in plastic bags in the listening center.

Children also need quiet, cozy spots to look at books, either alone or with a friend. Soft pillows, an overstuffed chair or sofa from a thrift store, and even a brightly painted refrigerator box create spaces where children can relax and unwind.

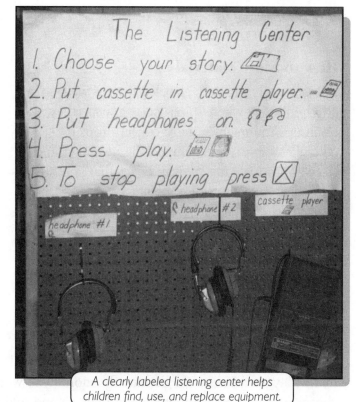

A clearly labeled listening center helps children find, use, and replace equipment.

Seeing themselves reflected in the books you select is comforting, so have a variety of published books that capture the ethnic and cultural backgrounds of all the children in the classroom. Children also want "their own books" in the class library. Any book you make with them—such as a photograph book of a class trip, books about the children, an alphabet book with contributions by each student—all belong in the library center.

Dramatic-Play Center

Possible Materials:

- Dolls and doll clothes
- Telephones
- Paper and pencils
- Board books for reading to the dolls
- Play medical supplies

- Dress-up clothes
- Briefcases
- Old computer keyboards
- Cooking and eating utensils
- Large hollow blocks

How to Store Materials:

All containers should be labeled here as well, so children know where things belong when they clean up. You might want to collect props for specific play themes, for example "the hospital," and store appropriate materials in boxes that you bring out when children ask for them.

At the beginning of the year, the dramatic-play center is often the most popular center. It is a place where many children can work through the stress of separating from home in a safe, familiar way. Props and costumes often give them the tools they need to work through their anxiety. Take Cassandra, for example. She had a difficult time separating from her mother on the first day of school, until she discovered the dramatic play area. There, she became the mommy at work. She put on high-heeled shoes, donned a pocketbook and a briefcase, and told everyone she "was going to her office." Once in her imaginary office space, she picked up the telephone, called home, and said, "Hi, dear, how are you? I miss you. I'll be back soon." Cassandra reassured herself by acting out what her mother was most likely thinking.

Teacher Tip

Stock Up on Props

Thrift stores are a great source for dramatic play props. Real telephones, briefcases, baby clothes, dolls, men's hats, women's purses, and so forth are inexpensive and so much more satisfying than props in school supply catalogs.

Arriving at Themes

As children begin to feel more at home in the classroom, the focus on family begins to fade. When this happens, introduce new props that will stimulate their imaginations and expand their play beyond the home. For example, bring out boxes of medical-related items such as surgical gowns, booties, gauze, and stethoscopes for playing hospital. Provide shoe boxes, a measuring device, a cash register, and pretend money for playing shoe store.

If you have room, consider adding large hollow blocks so that children can create buildings, furniture, and vehicles to support their dramatic play. Hollow blocks can become space ships, grocery-store shelves, office desks, hospital beds, or beauty-shop chairs. The sky's the limit.

Morning meeting is a good time to discuss dramatic play. If you ask children for settings and plots, they will brainstorm together. Prop boxes filled with theme-focused supplies can be used to encourage ideas. You can also involve children in making props to support a dramatic play theme of their choice.

Here are some ideas that have worked for teachers we've known:

The Magic Castle

In Ms. Dinerstein's kindergarten class, the students decided to turn their housekeeping corner into a magic castle. Together, they painted brown butcher paper to look like a brick wall and wrapped it around a wooden sink. They attached a pulley and string to the curved faucet, and hung a bucket (i.e., a small container wrapped in tin foil) down their "royal wishing well."

Using large pieces of brightly painted paper, they decorated two chairs as thrones for the king and queen. They made props for other characters as well; a knight's visor was constructed out of cardboard, tin foil, and strips of newspaper for the plume. The children covered dishes with tin foil to create fancy dinnerware and they produced several magic wands. The props took about two weeks to make. And every child made a contribution. As a result, they were eager to take turns dressing up and playing in their magic castle.

The Bookstore

After a visit to a local bookstore, Ms. Hayes's pre-K class decided to transform their dramatic play area into one of its own. The children gathered book catalogs from the store they visited, made their own signs, collected the class books they had made, built shelves from hollow blocks to put their books on display, and created the money for their customers. The store was open to parents each morning during

arrival time.

The children loved pretending to sell their homemade books because it gave them a sense of ownership. And since they had made all the props themselves, the entire bookstore truly belonged to them.

Tools for Keeping Track

In addition to taking notes, taking photographs and making books from them is an excellent way to document work in the dramatic-play center. When you ask children to tell you about their play, using your photographs as guides, they learn to organize and sequence their stories.

These books can also help children build shared memories of their work in the classroom. A book about the castle, for example, can be read and reread by children, teachers, and parents throughout the year, even long after the castle is gone. It's not unlike looking at a family photo album together. Reading these books is one more way to reinforce a child's sense of being at home in the classroom.

Establishing an Efficient Clean-Up Routine

Clean up is an important part of work time because it determines how quickly and easily children will be able to begin working at the center the next day. It also determines how quickly and easily children move to the next activity of the day. Introducing an efficient clean-up routine can be slow going at the beginning of the year, but spending time to build competence will pay off in the long run. Here are some ideas for establishing a routine:

Clean-Up Signals

To let children know that clean-up time is approaching, it's important to pick an easily identifiable signal to use near the end of work time. The room will be noisy because children are working in all the centers. A song, a bell, or even a xylophone may be difficult to hear. A better signal may be a flip of the lights. Have your students practice responding to the signal by stopping what they're doing and being silent. Tell them to look for you by the light switch and to listen for an important announcement. Then, let them know they have five more minutes until clean up.

When those five minutes are up, ask the child in charge of giving the official signal to do his job.

Quiet Signal

Some teachers prefer to use a "quiet signal," for example, holding up one hand and using the other to cover your mouth. When children see you using this signal, encourage them to do the same. From there, it should be quiet enough for everyone to hear whatever you need to say.

Clapping Patterns

Other teachers use a clapping pattern. At clean-up, you begin clapping out a rhythmic pattern. As the children hear it, they join in. Once everyone is clapping, ask the group to stop, then make your announcement.

Clean-Up Schedules

Sequenced Schedule

If your students need extra supervision to ensure a calm, organized clean up, you may want to have them all return to the rug at the signal. Then send them back to clean up with help from your assistant, one center at a time. While clean up is happening, the children waiting on the rug can sing songs, play simple guessing games, or share what they worked on. As each group finishes cleaning up, they rejoin the group on the rug until all centers are back in order. This sequenced clean-up method can avoid a lot of chaos.

Staggered Schedule

If your children don't need that kind of adult supervision, you may want to create a staggered schedule. With this system, children start cleaning up at different times, depending on the activity. If they worked in the meeting area, reading or playing with toys, they would be the first ones to start cleaning up, since most likely that space will be needed immediately following work time. Similarly, the block center and the dramatic-play center often require more clean-up time than other centers, and therefore children working at them should get an early start.

All children should know that after clean up, they are to return to the meeting area, where they can look at books or talk with friends while they wait for everyone to finish. With properly staggered clean-up time, no group should wait very long.

"Many Hands" System

Many hands lighten the load for everyone, and young children need to learn this for the common good of their class. So for areas that typically take more time to clean,

such as the block center, invite many children to help. Call the class back to the rug and ask everyone to do a small part. You can ask "toy collectors" to remove any accessories from buildings and return them to their labeled storage containers. Then send in a group of "stackers" who find blocks of similar shape, and stack them on the floor. Not only is this an efficient way to clean up centers, but it's also a great way to introduce children to sorting, classifying, and counting. Finally, send in the "shelvers" to finish the job. This system gives everyone an important job. And, by rotating small groups in and out of centers, there's always a manageable number of children within each one.

Once the children have worked, cleaned up, and perhaps shared their projects with one another at a brief meeting, they will be ready to move onto the next event in their day. The time they've spent engaged in activities of their own choosing has helped to solidify their feeling of being at home in the classroom. They have had opportunities to do things for themselves—to get what they need and return it on their own. These experiences will make it easier for them to move onto tasks that offer them less freedom to choose.

Chapter 6

Small-Group Instruction

Daily small-group instruction is essential, but finding the time to do it can be a problem. And solutions may vary, depending on children's ages.

Finding the Time in Pre-K

Pre-K children are often less able than school-aged children to carry out work that they haven't chosen to do. Therefore, conducting small-group instruction during work time, when the children select their activities, may be best. In small groups, you can:

★ **Introduce a New Activity.** It's easier to teach a new math game to a few students than to the whole class. Once everyone has had a chance to play the game in a small group, add it to the math center, so that children can play it on their own.

★ **Observe Each Child's Work Carefully.** When you play "alphabet bingo" with only four children, for example, it's easier to assess who needs help learning about letters.

★ **Integrate Subjects in a Fun, Engaging Context.** Cooking with a handful of children is a natural way to integrate math and reading skills. Children love to cook; creating a tasty snack for the entire class gives them a sense of mastery and self-accomplishment. But no four-or five-year-old could possibly wait for a turn if the whole class were cooking. Small groups are a must.

★ **Encourage Dialogue Among Children and Adults.** During a short trip to a grocery or hardware store, children will naturally question and discuss what they see. Your responses, as well as their classmates', will help them gain insights. Having personal exchanges is much more difficult with twenty children than it is with four or five.

If you notice a few children having difficulty with a task, such as recognizing letters or counting, design small-group activities to strengthen those skills. Select which children will participate, with you or an assistant leading the group. Use morning message to let them know who will be in small groups at work time. This provides a record of who's had a turn and who still needs one. You can also use your class list to keep track.

If you concentrate on a particular small group during work time, make sure your assistant is free to move around the room, watching what the other children are doing and helping them stay engaged. Your assistant may also need to respond to a variety of situations such as conflicts, spills, and technology malfunctions. If your assistant has difficulty trouble-shooting, assign her to small group while you attend to the other children.

Finding the Time in Kindergarten

For kindergarten children, separate small-group periods for literacy, math, social studies, and science, which last no more than thirty minutes, often work best. Most teachers wait until at least November, however, to insert these blocks into their daily schedules.

If you have an assistant, divide the class into three groups. Have one group work with you, one with your assistant, and one on its own, carrying out a clearly defined activity. If you have two assistants, either eliminate the independent group or break the class into four groups.

Once you have determined the composition of the groups, make charts so the children can keep track of where they belong. You might color code groups by name, for example the "blue group" with the children's names written in blue, the "red group" with the names written in red, and so on. Another option is to have each group adopt the name of one of the class pets, as Ms. Furman did. She also created a second chart that specified which teacher was working with which group each day.

Keeping Independent Workers Engaged

During small-group time, it's important that the "independent" group be just that—independent. Children must be fully engaged in a task that is easily accomplished without adult supervision. Here are some activities that work well:

★ **Write Around the Room.** Children move quietly around the room on a scavenger hunt for words. Their mission is to find words that start with a particular letter on hanging posters, displayed written work, objects, books, and other printed materials. Make sure the letter is one the children can recognize. When they find words, they

Name Ben	
Write all the 3 letter words you can find.	Job Max Art Our
Write all the 5 letter words you can find.	chart block write Snack April

Write around the room.

Forms like this help children work independently as you teach small groups.

write them down on a clipboard pad. They may be able to read none, some, or all of the words they find. Prepare clipboards in advance by using the reproducible form (see Appendix) or writing the beginning letter clearly on top of a blank piece of paper. Throughout the school year, you may need to increase the difficulty of this task by having children look for specific kinds of words, such as those with five letters or more.

★ **Pair Up and Read.** Children choose a traditional book from the class library or a recorded book from the listening center to enjoy alone or with a buddy.

★ **Man Those Manipulatives.** Using Unifix cubes, pattern blocks, or other manipulatives, children engage in independent, open-ended play for up to twenty minutes.

★ **Put It on Paper.** In homemade journals, children help each other write or draw whatever is on their minds. Be sure to give children the strategies they need to find the words they may want to use. Softcover glossaries containing basic, commonly used words are available in many school-supply stores. Using these glossaries or print sources that are posted around the classroom, children often find words they want to use. Also, encourage children to ask a friend for words and to listen for sounds in the words before attempting to put them on paper.

Scheduling Small Groups

How often should small-group work take place? If you've divided your class into three groups, consider scheduling three literacy periods and three math periods one week, saving social studies and science for the following week. On day one, introduce a skill to the first group while groups two and three work with an assistant or independently on other tasks. On day two, the first group practices the skill with your assistant, while you introduce the skill to the second group. On day three, your first group practices the skill independently, your second group practices it with the assistant, and your third group gets the introduction. By the end of the week, you will have introduced the skill to the entire class.

Choosing the Content

Now that you and your kindergarteners know when, where, and how small groups operate, what should you do in them? Literacy, mathematics, social studies, and science all lend themselves to small-group instruction. Here are some suggestions to get you started, as well as recommended books.

Literacy Activities

★ **ABCs.** Work with four or five children as they play alphabet games or put together alphabet puzzles. You can identify letters for them, demonstrate the sounds each letter makes, and discuss what words start with that letter. Your presence will help the children learn more than they would if they were playing alone.

★ **The Name Game.** Children love to play memory games. If they are beginning to recognize their own names and their classmates' in print, try this version of Concentration. Using small index cards, write the name of every child in your class on two cards. Then place the cards face down on a table. A child turns over two cards to see if they match. If they do, the cards remain face up. If they don't, the child places the cards face down again, and the next child takes a turn. Play continues until all matches have been found. If you have a particularly large class, you may want to limit the number of names, but be sure to include those of the children who are playing.

★ **Matchmaker, Matchmaker.** When children know their daily schedule and can read the schedule cards, here's another matching game to give them. (See Chapter 2 for more information on the daily schedule.) Reduce two copies of each schedule card so that they fit on three-by-five index cards. For extra support, glue the copies to the cards and laminate them or cover them with clear contact paper. Matchmaker, Matchmaker is played the same way as The Name Game: Ask children to take turns matching the periods in the daily schedule.

Reading self-made books is a wonderful use of small-group time.

★ **Book Club.** Gather children into a small group and read them a favorite book. This gives them the opportunity to follow the printed text closely, study the illustrations, and talk about the story more fully than they might in a larger group.

★ **Guided Reading.** By mid-year, many kindergarteners are ready for direct reading instruction. If you have multiple copies of leveled readers, you may want to use your literacy block for guided reading. For help in organizing and conducting groups, consult the teacher's guide that accompanies the leveled readers. It should contain detailed guidelines.

★ **Writing Circle.** Make plenty of blank books and keep them in the drawing and writing center. (See Chapter 5, page 49, for instructions on how to make blank books.) Gather children into a small group and have them tell you stories. Then, encourage them to write down their stories using invented spelling. For younger children, you may want to write their stories in blank books and ask them to illustrate them.

Teacher Tip

Get Started in Reading

For more small-group literacy activities, try:

Starting Out Right: A Guide to Promoting Children's Reading Success edited by Susan Burns, Peg Griffin, Catherine E. Snow (National Academy Press, 1998)

Phonics They Use: Words for Reading and Writing, Third Edition, by Patricia M. Cunningham (Addison-Wesley, 1999)

Teaching with Kids' Names by Bob Krech (Scholastic Teaching Resources, 2000)

Phonics Games Kids Can't Resist! Michelle K. Ramsey (Scholastic Teaching Resources, 2000)

Guided Reading: Making It Work by Mary Browning Schulman and Carleen daCruz Payne (Scholastic Teaching Resources, 2000)

Math Activities

★ **Number Books.** On small slips of paper, write numbers, from one to the total number of children in your class. Put the numbers in a hat. Let each child draw one. Then ask the children to circulate around the room, gathering a set of objects to represent their numbers, for example four pencils, six paint brushes, nine paper cups. Have each child arrange their items on a table and take a photo. Make a numbers book by gluing one photo per page to card stock and writing simple captions underneath each one, such as "Jeremy found 8 crayons." Laminate the covers and bind the book. The children will love reading and rereading them. If you don't want to keep the books from one year to the next, also include a photo of each child and give him his page to take home at year's end.

★ **Bingo.** Who doesn't love the thrill of shouting "Bingo"? For young children, Bingo can be modified to include only single-digit numbers. Later on, introduce double digits. Watching children play gives you an indication of which children need assistance recognizing written numbers.

A small group engaged in math activities.

★ **Board Games.** Familiar, simple games, such as Candy Land or Chutes and Ladders, not only teach children how to follow rules, but also help them learn colors and how to count as they proceed around the board.

★ **Fill Her Up!** Simple investigations show children the value of math in the everyday world. Start by giving them several small containers of different sizes to use at either the water or sand table. Ask them to help you figure out which containers hold more water or sand and which hold less. Using a measuring cup, have them fill containers one cup at a time. Each time they empty a cup, they should put a counter aside. When a container is full, have them total the counters to determine how many cups it took to fill the container. Write down what they discover and compare results.

★ **Racing Dice.** Photocopy the racing dice sheets at the back of the book. (See Appendix.) One sheet is for use with one die, the other for two dice. Children roll the die or dice. As numbers appear, children color, trace, and/or write in the corresponding column on the racing sheet, essentially making a bar graph that illustrates the frequency of appearances for each number. Children continue playing until the column representing one number is filled. That number wins. This game solidifies number recognition and numeral writing skills. By using two dice, you promote adding skills since the total number of dots must be determined to arrive at an answer.

Science Activities

Science is all around children, in the natural world. Center small-group instruction around accessible, understandable concepts, as well as steps in the scientific process, such as observing and recording. Here are ideas to adapt:

★ **Gardens.** In the spring, small groups can plant flower or vegetable seeds outdoors in your school's garden area. If your school doesn't have a garden area, plant the seeds in containers inside the classroom. Each group should have its own plot or container, which should be clearly labeled with the group's name. Children can monitor their seeds, keeping track of which ones sprout first, how many leaves appear on each stalk, which plant grows tallest, and how the plants are alike and different. Each week, have children measure their plants with string, transpose the measurement onto paper, and write the date below it. By transposing their measurements side by side, they will make a bar chart that illustrates growth. You can also take Polaroid photos of the plants over time, or have children draw them, to document growth. Again, be sure to date each installment.

★ **Pet Studies.** If you have pets in the classroom, gather a small group together to look carefully at them. Get the children to describe what they see by asking questions such as, "What kind of fur or skin does this animal have?" "Does it have a tail?" "Is it long or short?" "Does it have legs?" "How does it use them?" "Where are its eyes?" "How does it eat?" and so on. As the children share their observations, encourage them to draw what they see. You can also chart the

characteristics of one or more animals and ask the children to discuss what makes them similar to and different from one another.

★ **Simple Experiments.** Small groups are great for introducing and testing out simple scientific concepts. Give group members a set of different objects, such as a pencil, a plastic cup, a marble, and a feather, and ask them to find out which float and which sink in water. Have them record their results on an observation sheet. (See Appendix.) Ask them to describe each object: what it looks like, how it feels. Then ask, "Why do you think these things sank?" "Why do you think these floated?" "How are they similar or different?" As the children characterize each object, make a list of properties they come up with.

★ **Playground Laboratory.** The school playground can serve as the perfect nature laboratory. Depending on the season, you might take a small group of children there to explore insect life, observe the effect of sunlight on puddles, record how trees change, or document plant growth.

Social Studies Activities

Young children are eager to learn about the world around them. Taking short trips into the neighborhood is a great way to enrich your curriculum and provide hands-on learning experiences.

★ **Visiting Local Businesses.** Stores, repair shops, restaurants, gas stations, and other neighborhood businesses are valuable places to investigate. Make arrangements in advance so that proprietors and employees expect the visit and will welcome the children. By encouraging children to ask questions of the people who work there, you encourage them to do research. As they see how businesses work, they will begin to understand how the separate strands are woven together to create a community.

★ **Sketch the Neighborhood.** A simple stroll around the block holds incredible wonders for young children. Equipped with drawing paper, clipboards, and pencils, encourage them to observe and illustrate the different types of buildings they see. Have them study doorways, rooflines, windows, and other architectural details, as well as the materials used to construct the buildings. Along the way, children may notice other things, such as birds on a telephone pole, which might lead to an examination of the poles themselves: Where do the wires go? Why are there so many wires? What do the signs on the poles say?

★ **Interview Members of the Community.** Some whole-group experiences, like riding the bus to school, may provide inspiration for small-group studies. During meeting time, you might ask the children what they know about school buses and their drivers. Help them pinpoint what they're not sure of and what questions they have. Take small groups to interview the bus driver. The children might ask, "How did you learn to drive?" "How do you know where we live?" "How long does it take you to drive your route each morning?" "Who fixes the bus when it breaks?" "How do you open the door?" and "What makes the stop sign extend?" Ask each group to share what it learned with the whole class sometime after the interview.

★ **Research the School.** If you can't venture beyond school grounds, engage the children in a study of the building itself. With a little imagination, this can provide months of valuable investigations. You and your assistant might take turns helping small groups

- map the school's hallway
- count the number of classrooms in the school
- find out how many children attend the school
- research how many pets live in the building

Teacher Tip

Enlist Volunteers for Field Trips

When you take the entire class on a trip, make sure you have enough parent volunteers to divide the class into small groups, with one adult for every five to seven children.

Share with the parents the questions the children generated beforehand, so that they can help the children find answers. Also, remind parents to ask the children open-ended questions, such as, "What do you notice about the ostrich?" rather than "Who knows what that's called?" If you give each adult a clipboard and pencil, they can write down what the children tell them.

As you decide on the composition of groups, remember that you and your assistant should be in charge of children who require the most assistance to stay focused and behave appropriately.

- interview employees of the school

- explore areas that they typically don't visit, such as the furnace room or the principal's office

- talk with someone who went to the school many years before

Make sure to bring along plenty of paper, sharpened pencils, and clipboards, so you and the children can draw and write about what you see. When the group returns to the classroom, start a conversation with members about their experiences and ask them to draw and write about the trip. When everyone has had a chance to explore, collect the children's work and make a book about the school.

After working in small-groups, it's time for a break. Snack time allows children to refuel their bodies and spirits. Healthy snacks are a must. And unless you're serving something no one likes, you won't need a great deal of motivation to move the children toward the table or into their chairs.

Explore Your World

For more small-group social studies activities, try these:

Explorations with Young Children: A Curriculum Guide from the Bank Street College of Education by Anne Mitchell and Judy David (Gryphon House, 1992)

Social Studies for the Preschool-Primary Child, Fifth Edition, by Carol Seefeldt (Merrill, 1996)

Classroom Interviews: A World of Learning (book and video) by Paula Rogovin (Heinemann, 1998)

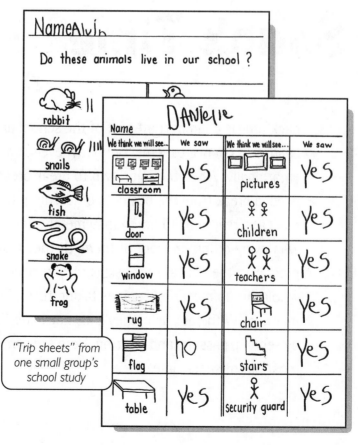

"Trip sheets" from one small group's school study

Chapter 7

Snack Time

Snack time is an important part of the school day because it gives children a chance to refuel on many levels: physically, socially, and emotionally. When they sit down to break bread, they get a much-needed break from the business of learning. This is their time to relax and revitalize. Children may merely stare into space, devouring whatever you put in front of them. Or they may talk informally, practicing the critical social skills they've been gaining during whole-group meetings, such as taking turns, listening, using manners. With your help, they'll also develop fine-motor skills by serving, passing, and pouring. Here are some ways to get the most out of snack time.

Scheduling

If your class has lunch around noon, it's best to schedule a snack for mid-morning. But if lunch happens mid- to late-morning, as some do, then schedule snack time in the afternoon. For children who stay in the classroom past three o'clock, serving another snack in the late afternoon is a good idea. Regardless of when you schedule snack time, allow about twenty minutes so the children have ample time to converse, eat, and clean up.

Setting Up

Once you've decided on the right time for snacks, assign helpers to set the tables and distribute food. If you use a job chart, your helpers will be able to identify themselves easily. (See Chapter 2, pages 22–23, for more information on job charts.) They'll also take pride in providing a service that benefits everyone.

Snack helpers usually need adult supervision to set up. Give them cups and napkins and ask them to place a setting in front of each chair at the tables. As children match the number of settings to the number of chairs, they develop an awareness of one-to-one correspondence. If you hand them the incorrect number of cups or napkins, talk to them about why they have shortages or leftovers. This helps to develop number sense.

Once the tables are set, snack helpers can set out baskets of crackers or small paper cups of applesauce, soup, or rice. It may be difficult for them to pour juice from big cans into smaller pitchers, so assist them. If six or more children are at a table, make at least two baskets and pitchers available. Young children can wait, but not for long!

To give snack helpers the time and space to do their jobs, have another adult read a story to the rest of the class in the meeting area, away from the tables, before snack time begins.

Get Down to Basics

Discount and dollar stores are good sources for basic supplies such as baskets, plastic utensils, small pitchers, and paper goods.

Make "snack helper" a rotating classroom
job to build children's independence.

Once snack time begins, foster children's growing independence by letting them take their own crackers from the baskets and pour their own juice from the pitchers. (If pitchers are too heavy, use plastic two-cup measuring cups.) Be prepared for spills, and let the children know it's okay if they have an accident, as long as they help clean up. So, be sure they know where sponges are kept. It's tempting to do all of these things for children to save time. But, rest assured, allowing them to be independent is time well spent.

What's the Snack?

What you serve can be as simple as crackers and juice or as complicated as homemade muffins and fresh-squeezed orange juice. If you have appliances in your classroom, as well as the time, desire, and license to cook with children, the snack menu can vary considerably. Whenever possible, make things from scratch. That way, you tap into the educational value of cooking as children learn to cut, chop, measure, combine, mix, blend, stir, and so forth.

If you have a convection, microwave, or toaster oven at your disposal, you can do a lot of baking. If you only have a hotplate, you can still cook many different types of rice, soup, and vegetables. And your classroom will smell delicious all year long. If you have none of these small appliances, don't despair; there are many delicious no-bake recipes, too.

A well-stocked, accessible cooking center

Get Cooking

Cooking is reading, math, and science all rolled into one. By doing it in small groups, you can introduce many important skills: reading for specific purposes, measuring ingredients, and observing how properties change as concoctions are mixed, blended, baked, boiled, roasted, fried, or frozen.

Select recipes yourself and invite children to bring some from home. After gathering the ingredients you need, read the recipe aloud from a chart. To help younger children decode the text, make sure pictures represent procedures clearly.

If you carefully label containers, shelves, and racks, older children should be able to find what they need on their own. With permanent colored markers, label

measuring cups and spoons, for example green for 1/2, red for 1/4. Use the same color-coding system on recipes, so children can determine amounts easily.

After you've finished cooking, review the recipe. Children will delight in knowing what they did first, next, and last. Best of all, cooking is a natural way for children to nurture one another. When they take turns preparing a snack for the whole group, they care for one another in an important, grown-up way.

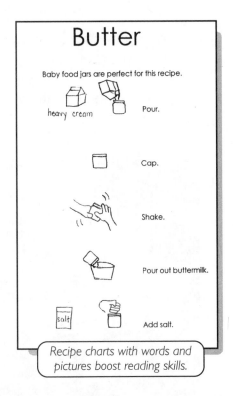

Butter

Baby food jars are perfect for this recipe.

heavy cream — Pour.

Cap.

Shake.

Pour out buttermilk.

salt — Add salt.

Recipe charts with words and pictures boost reading skills.

Make Your Own Snacks

Here are some snack ideas organized by the appliances you'll need to carry them out:

Hotplate or Stove:

★ **Applesauce.** After making a large quantity of basic applesauce, have one group add honey, have another add cinnamon, another brown sugar, and so on. That way, each group will have an opportunity to "cook" applesauce in a different way. After you've prepared all varieties, have children record their taste preferences in a classroom graph.

Teacher Tip

Find Appropriate Appliances

You don't need a gourmet kitchen to cook in your classroom. Any or all of these appliances will work just fine:

- stove
- convection oven
- hotplate
- toaster oven
- blender
- crockpot

★ **Rice.** Rice is a wonderful snack, particularly if you live in a cold climate. Try basmati rice, brown rice, short grain rice, long grain rice, rice and beans, rice with butter, rice with grated cheese, fried rice, rice pudding, and so on. You might even introduce children to chopsticks.

★ **Soup.** Cooking soup from scratch is great fun. It requires advance planning, but the aroma alone makes it worth the trouble. You and the children might sample vegetable soup, noodle soup, carrot soup, pumpkin soup, chicken soup, potato soup, and so many others.

Conventional, convection, or toaster oven:

★ **Bread.** There are an infinite number of breads. Quick breads are easier to make than yeast breads. But the experience of kneading dough, watching it rise, and smelling it bake makes yeast breads worth the effort. Bread is also a great focus for a theme study on different cultures.

★ **Muffins.** Corn, blueberry, bran, and raisin—all are inviting and easy to make.

★ **Birthday Cakes.** Allow children to make their own cake on their birthday. The birthday child can choose two helpers, one for baking and one for icing. The entire class enjoys their creation.

Electric Frying Pan:

★ **French Toast or Pancakes.** Serve them with homemade applesauce instead of sugary syrup.

★ **Eggs.** Be sure to thoroughly cook the yoke, given recent health warnings.

★ **Grilled Cheese Sandwiches.** Cut them into quarters and experiment with different kinds of breads and cheeses.

Blender:

★ **Smoothies.** Mix together fruit and juices for a tasty drink.

★ **Yogurt Shakes.** Add yogurt to a fruit smoothie.

★ **Homemade Peanut Butter.** Shell peanuts and blend them with a little oil until smooth.

★ **Chilled Vegetable and Fruit Soups.** Check a good cookbook for soups that don't require cooking.

Check Out These Recipe Sources

The cookbooks on your kitchen shelf may contain many recipes you can make with the children. You may even have some written especially for children. Here are a few to consider:

The Children's Kitchen Garden: A Book of Gardening, Cooking and Learning by Georgeanne Brennan and Ethel Brennan (Ten Speed Press, 1997)

Let's Get Cooking by Margot Hammond Lancaster (Childcraft, 1998)

Cooking Without a Stove: A Cookbook for Young Children by Aileen Paul (Sunstone Press, 1987)

The Good Housekeeping Illustrated Children's Cookbook by Marianne Zanzarell (Morrow Jr. Books, 1997)

If you can't cook with children, you can vary snacks by squeezing different kinds of fruit to make juices. Smear cream cheese, hummus, and other spreads on crackers or bread. Put the spreads in small, individual cups so the children can serve themselves, using plastic knives. You could also offer grapes, popcorn, or raisins, which can also be served in cups, one cup per child.

Getting the Food You Need

If your school does not fund snack time, supporting it yourself is a challenge. Some teachers ask parents for a small monthly or quarterly donation. If that isn't possible, send home a list of food items you would like parents to donate. (See Appendix.) Some teachers have received mini-grants from their school districts to finance their cooking curriculum.

Avoid serving sweets. Cookies may be inexpensive, but pretzels or crackers are more nutritious, and cost just as little. Also, discourage parents from sending their child to school with his own snack, since it tends to create conflict. Children who aren't given "good" snacks envy those who are. And if children offer to share their "good" snacks with just a few special friends, then the other children feel left out.

Dear Parents,

Our snack program is underway. We have been enjoying a variety of snacks such as crackers, popcorn, and corn muffins.

The children enjoy preparing the snacks as they gain self-confidence and important skills such as measuring, estimating, reading a recipe, following directions, and sequencing, just to name a few.

As the year progresses there are some items we will need. I have prepared a request form. I would appreciate your cooperation in sending in the needed item. Requests will be sent on a rotating basis so everyone will have a turn to participate.

Through your donations, your child will also benefit by feeling as though they are making a contribution to their classroom community.

Thank you for your cooperation.

Sincerely,
Mrs. Furman

By carving out time for a daily snack—a special time in which everyone sits, talks, and enjoys the same food—children will surely feel more at home in the classroom.

Not everyone finishes eating at the same time. Therefore, children who are speedy need to know exactly what they should do after their snack. Here are some possibilities:

★ Get coats to get ready for outside play

★ Go to the meeting area and look at books

★ Make a choice for work time and get started

★ Listen to music in preparation for rest

Chapter 8

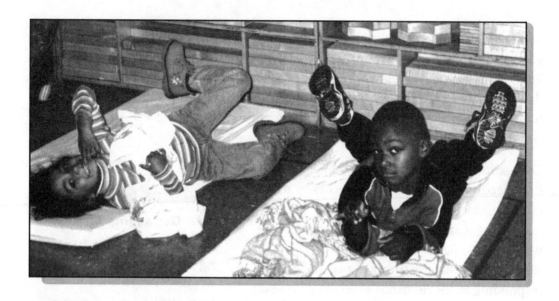

Rest Time

Young children tire easily. Rest is often the only time during the school day when they can relax, make up for lost sleep, and recover from the work of socializing with so many peers.

Settling children down can be a challenge. Often they find it difficult to lie still and be quiet among friends or in a place other than home. But rest is essential in pre-K and kindergarten, and it's up to you to make sure all the children get about forty-five minutes of it a day.

Before we share suggestions about how to help children rest, though, we want to clarify why rest is so important. You've probably heard parents ask, "Why do you let the children sleep when they could be doing something important like learning the alphabet?" Convincing parents that children should rest may be your first big challenge.

Why Rest?

Young children need a lot of sleep. Often, they don't get enough at night. They may go to bed late or be awoken by bad dreams, street noise, the crying of a younger sibling, or any number of things. Whatever the reason, children should nap during the day. Just as we give children a good breakfast because food ensures they will function well, we must apply the same thinking to their need for sleep. Tired children simply cannot perform effectively in the classroom.

Over-stimulation is another reason young children need sleep. Being around twenty or more other children in a small space all day can be exhausting. Children's senses are bombarded with sounds, sights, smells, and so on. Resolving conflicts, learning to play together, responding to the demands of adults who also must consider the needs of the whole group—it's all hard work. During the day, children crave a "time out" that isn't punitive, a chance to be alone with their thoughts. Even if they don't fall asleep, rest period frees them from the all-consuming demands of structured activity and social interaction.

Not all children need to sleep, however, and some are totally unfazed by social demands. These children's needs must also be considered. Constantly trying to keep active children still and quiet can make you and them feel anything but relaxed! Here are some suggestions to help make rest productive for everyone.

Teacher Tip

Get a Jump on Rest

Before the school year begins, during a home visit or an orientation, discuss the importance of rest period with parents. If you can't have a face-to-face meeting with them, send home a note that explains when rest period occurs, what children lie on, and what objects they should send in with their children to help them feel more secure—small blankets, stuffed animals, and so forth. If possible, ask parents about their child's sleeping habits. This kind of initial assessment will help you identify the children who may have difficulty napping or resting peacefully.

The ABCs of Catching Some ZZZs

There aren't many children who can fall asleep anytime or anywhere. At the beginning of the year, encourage children to bring a soft toy and small blanket from home, to help them feel secure. Most children will choose to leave a security object at school. Some, however, may choose to shuttle their very favorite object between home and school. That's okay, as long as they are reminded to bring it in each day.

Storing Security Toys and Blankets ☼

Where you store these objects is important. Many state and local health departments require teachers to store children's blankets separately. If children have individual cubbies, use them as safe, hygienic spots for blankets and toys. But if they don't, or if they share one cubby, you'll need to store their security objects elsewhere. Small, drawstring bags are a good option. If you sew, you can create them from fabrics such as denim or heavy cotton. Just attach a label with the child's name to the drawstring. These bags can be washed and used year after year. If you don't sew, use paper shopping bags or more durable string shopping bags.

Consider storing toys and blankets in sturdy drawstring bags.

Preparing for Rest ☼

Finding enough space for children to lie down may be a problem, too, especially if you have a small room. But if they clean up well after morning work time, you can use the block and meeting areas for rest.

You may want to assign rest spots. That way, children who have difficulty relaxing during rest can be kept apart from the others. If you allow children to choose their own spot, however, make it clear that you will move them if they bother the children around them.

Children can set up for rest, as long as they have adult supervision. Let the day's "mat helpers" assist you in laying out and putting away the mats. (For more information on class jobs, see Chapter 2.) If rest is scheduled just after lunch, have mat helpers set up at the start of lunch, so they have plenty of time to eat as well. When lunch is over, all the children can get their blankets and toys, and move to their mats.

But if your children eat early, as many kindergartners must, you'll need to choose a different pre-rest activity. You may want children to gather in the meeting area for a story, while another adult assists the mat helpers. Mats for those resting in the meeting area can be set up after the story, when children leave to collect their toys and blankets.

Teacher Tip

Use All-Purpose Mats

Asking children to rest at their desks is neither practical nor comfortable. To really relax, they need to lie down.

We prefer giving them mats over an unpadded rug or clunky cots. Try to buy durable, thick ones, enough for each child. Storing them can be a challenge. Closets, shelves, empty room corners—leave no space unturned in your quest for the perfect solution.

Setting the Mood

Lower the shades, turn off the lights in stages, put soothing music on your tape or CD player, and ask children to use their "quiet" voices as they settle down. Don't expect children to stop talking right away; give them time to slide gradually into the silence of rest. Say things such as, "In five minutes, it will be time to stop talking" or "In two more minutes, I'm going to turn off the last light, and then it will be time to stop talking."

After turning off the last light, circulate around the room. Offer to cover children with their blankets. Remind anxious children that they don't have to fall asleep, but they must rest

All-purpose mats are comfortable and easy to store.

quietly. You may want to confer with parents about methods they use to calm their children at home. For example, one little girl, Sandra, had been especially restless. During the initial weeks of school, she chatted, squirmed, and prevented others from falling asleep. After a brief conversation with Sandra's mother, the teacher learned that rubbing Sandra's back was part of her bedtime routine. So the teacher tried it. She began rest time by sitting on the floor next to Sandra and gently massaging her back. From that point on, Sandra would fall asleep within minutes.

You might also try reading chapter books to the non-sleepers, since hearing your soft, familiar voice may help them relax. Explain that during rest time you read stories quietly and without showing the pictures. Encourage children to create pictures in their minds as you read. And be sure to find books you love because if you enjoy reading them, chances are the children will enjoy hearing them.

After you've read for twenty to twenty-five minutes, walk around the room and give any remaining children who are awake picture books or magazines to look at on their own. You might also consider giving them small puzzles or buckets containing Legos, table blocks, or connecting cubes. Just be sure to tell them to play quietly because other children are still sleeping.

Once the class has settled down, it may be tempting to do paperwork or talk with your colleagues, but don't. Rest happens when children are confident that you are paying attention to them.

Ending Rest

Some children may still be fast asleep at the end of rest. You'll have to decide whether it's in their best interest to wake them or to let them sleep on. The conversation with parents about the child's home sleeping habits should help you here, as will your own observations about the child's behavior, mood and energy that day. If

you do let a child continue sleeping, move his mat to an out-of-the-way spot in the classroom. If he is a heavy sleeper, the movement shouldn't wake him. Even noise from the woodworking bench shouldn't!

Children who are ready to rise will need assistance in putting things away. Mat helpers should be called first, so they can help you or your assistant store the mats. Then ask the rest of the children to put away their security objects. Calling on only a few at a time prevents traffic jams.

Once they've put their things away, children need to know what to do or where to go. If work time follows rest, you may want them to gather on the rug for a brief meeting to discuss which centers they'd like to work in. Or ask them to come and tell you where they want to work. Once you've approved each child's choice, have him indicate it on the choice board and get to work.

If rest is followed by a whole-group activity such as music, gym, or story time, children who rise quickly will need something to do, while their classmates reorient themselves. Since this is a transition time, don't offer choices that require extensive clean up. Looking at books, drawing pictures, writing with friends are all good options. When everyone is up, have the quick-risers put away their materials quickly and move on.

Chapter 9

Full-Group Instruction

or children in preschool and kindergarten, the school day is often made up of a series of choices—what center to work in, what materials to work with, what small group to join, and so on. There should be time, however, when the entire class works together. We covered morning meeting in Chapter 4. In this chapter, we address story time, shared reading, and modeled writing. As with small-group instruction, full-group periods should be short. Twenty or thirty minutes is usually time enough for young children.

Story Time

Children who hear many books read aloud are more likely to become better readers than those who don't. That's why we advocate reading stories to the whole class every day.

Gather children in the meeting area for story time. Make sure they all can see the book from where they are sitting by aligning them in rows facing you or fanning them out in a semicircle.

An excellent picture book is a marriage of well-written text and wonderful illustrations, which should be heard and seen simultaneously. So hold the book in one hand at shoulder height, so that the inside spreads face the children, and turn the pages with your free hand. That way, everyone will be able to enjoy the illustrations as you read the text. Of course, the more familiar you are with the text, the easier it will be for you to read and display the book all at once.

Introduce a story by explaining why you picked it. For example, you might say, "This book is about a pumpkin, which we are going to be studying in class," or "This is one of my favorite stories about a bear named Corduroy," or even "This book is a rhyming book that talks about all the feelings we have." Then you might say, "Now, we are going to read the story and wait until the end to discuss it."

The first time you read a story, it's best to go straight through without stopping to discuss the plot or difficult words since interruptions will make it harder for children to remember the story's sequence. Instead, read on, letting the plot's tension build to a satisfying conclusion. When you finish, pause for a moment of collective enjoyment and then begin your discussion.

Before you engage children in a discussion about a book, plan open-ended questions—ones with many possible answers—ahead of time. Although many children may know the answer to closed questions, only one of them will get to tell it, which will leave others feeling frustrated and excluded. Instead of inviting healthy talk about books, closed questions only create competition among students for the right answer. Asking open-ended questions leads to more inclusive conversations in which children listen and talk to one another. After reading Maurice Sendak's *Where the Wild Things Are*, for instance, you might ask:

★ **"Why do you think Max was being so wild?"** This question allows children to think about the times they have been wild—or wanted to be. It helps them to identify with the story's main character. Like all good writers, Sendak leaves

certain things unexplained; he doesn't tell us why Max was behaving like a wild thing. It's up to the readers, the children, to respond by filling in their own ideas.

★ **"In the story, Max traveled to a place filled with wild things. Why do you think he wasn't afraid of them?"** This question raises issues of power, something children are eager to explore. Like Max, they often feel powerless and want to be more in control. As they discuss Max's relationship with the wild things, the children may disagree with one another. This gives you an opportunity to help them listen to one another and share their own ideas, without hurting one another's feelings. It's a skill we all need to practice.

★ **"How did Max know how to find his home when he sailed back in his boat?"** A question like this invites children to think about the nature of the story. Was it the story of a dream? Or is Max magical and the story "real"? Young children often wrestle with the notions of fantasy and reality. It's important to ask questions that help them verbalize what they think.

★ **"Who left the supper in Max's room? Do you think Max saw a person bring the food?"** This question also addresses the notion of fantasy and/or reality. Some might believe that Max really went to some other place. Others will argue that he was in his room the whole time, wishing he could run far away, and that he saw his mother bring in his dinner. Still others might aptly suggest that Max dreamed his journey, and didn't see his mother bring in the dinner because he was asleep.

You can encourage children to share their own ideas by asking, "Does anyone have a question about the story that we haven't already talked about?" During the discussion, children will often make connections between something that happened in the story and something that happened in their own lives. Make sure to allow time for such comments.

Finding Good Stories ☀

There are many wonderful stories to read, but finding them isn't always easy. If your school does not have a large library, use your public library and ask the children's librarian for help. Chances are, she will be eager to show you her favorite books. She will probably also point out an excellent reference: Carolyn W. Lima's *A to Zoo: Subject Access to Children's Picture Books*, Fifth Edition, an extensive listing of children's books organized by subject, author, and title. The following resources, by the Children's Book Committee at Bank Street College of Education, will also help you locate books:

• *The Best Children's Books of the Year*, published annually

- *Books to Read Aloud with Children of All Ages*

To order these references, write to the Children's Book Committee, Bank Street College of Education, 610 West 112th Street, New York, NY 10025, or call (212) 875-4540.

Shared Reading

Shared reading is another essential form of whole-group instruction. In addition to complete stories, you'll find that short rhymes, simple poems, or silly song lyrics are ideal. You might want to start with Mother Goose rhymes. Write them on chart paper and ask children to read along with you as you read them aloud, indicating each word on the chart.

Patterned stories, which contain repeated lines or phrases similar to the refrains of a song, are another good choice. Eric Carle, for example, repeats the line, "But he was still hungry!" throughout *The Very Hungry Caterpillar*. Bill Martin repeats the title throughout *Brown Bear, Brown Bear, What Do You See?* It won't take children long to learn the pattern, and they will love chiming in with key responses or familiar refrains. Both books are in libraries and bookstores. For more ideas about how to use patterned books, see *Getting the Most from Predictable Books: Strategies & Activities for Teaching With More Than 75 Favorite Children's Books* by Michael F. Opitz (Scholastic Teaching Resources, 1996).

When you help children memorize the words to poems, songs, and stories, you are giving them a common language. When you ask them to join in a choral reading, you are solidifying your classroom community. For children, "knowing the words" makes them feel that they belong.

Modeled Writing

Children learn a lot through modeling—watching and imitating adult behavior. By modeling writing, you can help children acquire knowledge of consonant and vowel sounds, as well as letter formations. Here are some examples of how kindergarten teacher Lenore Furman modeled writing for her whole class:

Ms. Furman's School Study

The children in Ms. Furman's kindergarten class were studying their school. To learn about the jobs there, they decided to interview employees throughout the building. Before an interview, Ms. Furman asked the children what questions they might have and wrote them down on a large piece of chart paper. For the security guard, for example, Juan Carlos wanted to know why he wore a uniform. Michael wondered if he had a gun. Crystal wondered if he were the boss of the school.

As each child voiced a question, Ms. Furman repeated his words, and then asked the whole class to help her listen for the initial sounds in each word. As the children identified the letters that matched the sounds, she wrote down the words.

Modeled writing supported and extended the children's awareness of the relationship between the sounds they hear and the letters in words they speak, write, and read. And because Ms. Furman used the children's own words, they were more likely to remember what she wrote.

Ms. Furman also wrote each child's name next to his question, sending a strong message that children's ideas belong to them and that individual voices within the group were to be heard and respected.

After the whole-group meeting, the children conducted their interviews during small-group periods. In addition to the security guard, they visited the nurse, the principal, and the custodian. At end-of-day meetings, groups that had completed their interviews shared them with their classmates. As they did, Mrs. Furman wrote the answers next to their original questions on the chart paper.

Our Name Study

A name study is another whole-group activity that will engage your children. Pat Cunningham describes this exercise in her book, *Phonics They Use: Words for Reading & Writing*, Third Edition (Addison-Wesley, 1999). Each day, before class, choose one of the children's first names and make individual cards representing each letter in the name. Gather the children, hand out the letter cards randomly, and write the name on chart paper. Be sure to write slowly and large enough for everyone to see.

Capture Every Photo Opportunity

Photograph your students frequently. If you have an aide or adult volunteer, appoint her photographer. The image inventory you create will prove handy for all your book-making projects.

Then ask the child whose name it is to organize her classmates holding cards into the correct spelling of her name. For example, if the child's name is Emily, five children stand in front of the group and hold up their letter cards for all to see. Emily then moves those children around, unscrambling the letters, until her name is spelled correctly. She should use the chart as a reference if necessary.

As children become familiar with one another's names, they will begin to make comparisons between their names and their classmates'. "I have an 'e' in my name, too," one child might say. "But it isn't at the beginning like it is in Evan's."

After a child's name is spelled out, invite her to sit in front of the group to be interviewed. As children ask questions, write out her answers on chart paper, creating a "story": "Emily has two sisters and one brother. She's the oldest. She has a pet cat named Blackie and she feeds him every day. Emily went to pre-school with Evan and Amanda, and she loves building with blocks." Then ask the children to write Emily's

This is Brianna. She likes strawberry ice cream and chocolate chip cookies. She eats Spaghettio's too. Pink is Brianna's favorite color. Her house is made of red bricks. She lives with her mommy Gina, Lenny and her brother Justin.

Brianna doesn't have any pets but she has a robot dog named Tekno.

Pages from Brianna's book, which evolved from a name study

name at the top of a blank piece of paper and draw a picture of her. Collect the pictures and transfer her story onto similar-sized paper. Create a book about the child by placing the story and pictures between two pieces of construction paper and binding the left edge. If you've taken the child's photo during the school year, consider affixing it to the book's cover.

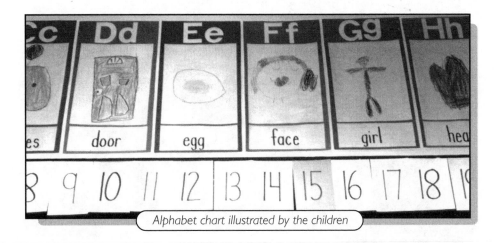

Alphabet chart illustrated by the children

By the time you've finished studying each child's name, children will have learned the sounds of many letters, honed some basic interviewing skills, and gained self-worth because they were at the heart of the curriculum.

The school study and the name study are firmly linked to what matters most to children—themselves and their world. Talking about unfamiliar places, such as Peru, will not hold children's attention unless, of course, a child has just come back from a trip there or is of South American descent. But the studies outlined in this chapter will keep them engaged because they put information within reach and enable children to make discoveries through first-hand experience.

Teacher Tip

Chart the Alphabet

Learning about the alphabet is most productive when there's choice involved. Here's a fun way for kindergartners to make their own class alphabet chart. Put lots of "ABC" books and age-appropriate dictionaries in your writing center. Have each child choose a letter and draw a picture of a word that begins with it. The letter *B*, for instance, might inspire a picture of a bathtub. Encourage children to draw the objects large enough for everyone to see from a distance. Once each child has contributed, write the name of the object under the picture, add its upper- and lower-case initial letter above (*B, b*), and string the pictures together.

After all this head work, it's time to work the body. The period following whole-group instruction is a good time for children to run, jump, and play outdoors. Most likely, you won't need to motivate them; they'll be eager for a change of pace.

Chapter 10

Outside Play

When you plan your daily schedule, be sure to allot at least thirty minutes each day to outdoor activities. Children need the space and freedom to run, shout, climb, or huddle together.

Some teachers arrange outdoor time for mid-morning or even early morning to give children a chance to use up some physical energy in preparation for more focused indoor activities. Others schedule it after rest, when children need a release after being still and quiet. And some teachers have no control over the decision.

Regardless of when you go out, be sure that you all go out, because learning doesn't end at the door. In fact, recess is prime teaching time! Young children need you to teach them how to play respectfully with one another and help them to resolve conflicts. They love to create worlds of their own, so encourage imaginative play. Also, support their attempts at challenging themselves.

Ready, Set, Go!

Clothing

It's not always easy getting young children ready to play outside, especially if you live where coats, mittens, hats, and boots are needed for months on end, but it's worth it. Urge children to help one another bundle up, and encourage their parents to send them to school dressed for outdoor play, even on the most inclement of days.

Equipment

Some schools have spacious, fully equipped playgrounds with swings, slides, and climbing structures. If yours is one of them, encourage children to use everything the playground has to offer. But be sure to give them your support and protection as they cross those bars, hang upside down from them, and so forth.

If your playground doesn't have permanent equipment, consider creating your own with the children. Use simple materials like planks and hollow blocks to construct enclosures. A local lumberyard or classroom supply store may sell these materials. Buy planks made from wood specifically treated for the outdoors. To weatherize the blocks, apply a clear coat of child-safe stain.

Teacher Tip

Keep "Extras" on Hand

Keep a bag for extra clothes handy. That way, if children come to school without an item, such as mittens, you'll have a spare pair. If they get their socks wet outside, you'll have a clean, dry pair waiting for them, while their own dry out. Warm sweat pants work equally well for boys and girls. Your local thrift shop is a great source for children's extras. You can also ask parents to send in old clothes for the bag.

And don't forget the basics such as balls, jump ropes, bubbles, and sidewalk chalk. Four-year-olds require lots of assistance when learning to jump rope, but five-year-olds can usually master it with just a bit of help. Use the chalk for hopscotch, running games, and outdoor masterpieces.

Games

In the fall, when children don't yet know one another well, you might have to spend time helping them play together. Try simple games like *Duck, Duck, Goose*. Children sit in a circle, and one child is designated as "it." That child walks around the outside of the circle, tapping each child's head, calling either "Duck" or "Goose." If she calls "Duck," no one in the circle moves. But when she chooses a "Goose," she must run around the circle while the Goose chases her. If the tapper makes it all the way around and sits down in the Goose's empty spot before being tagged, the Goose then becomes "it" and the game begins again. If, however, the Goose tags the tapper before she can sit down, the Goose takes a seat and the tapper remains "it."

Here are a few other outdoor group games: *Freeze Tag; Red Rover, Red Rover; 1-2-3 Red Light; Simon Says;* and *Mother, May I.* Once you've taught them the rules, most children will be able to play them on their own.

Teacher Tip

Have a Ball

If you're running short of play balls, make your own. Just take a child's sock, fill it with rice, tie it tightly with sturdy string, and you've got a ball that's easy to throw and catch.

Teacher Tip

Let the Games Begin

If your children have a gym class during the week, you might want to extend what they're learning into recess time. If they don't have a gym class, or if you're simply looking for more great games, consult these books:

Jump, Wiggle, Twirl, and Giggle: 25 Easy and Irresistible Movement Activities by Roberta Altman (Scholastic Teaching Resources, 2000)

Pathways to Play: Developing Play Skills in Young Children by Sandra Heidemann and Deborah Hewitt (Redleaf Press, 1992)

New Games for the Whole Family by Dale N. LeFevre (Perigree Books, 1988)

Hopscotch, Hangman, Hot Potato, & HA HA HA: A Rulebook of Children's Games by Jack Maguire (Fireside Press, 1990)

The Outside Play and Learning Book: Activities for Young Children by Karen Miller (Gryphon House, 1989)

Jump for Joy: Over 375 Creative Movement Activities for Young Children by Myra K. Thompson (Parker Publishing, 1993)

Keeping a Close Watch

By supervising the playground closely, not only will you keep children out of harm's way, you'll learn a great deal about their behaviors, personalities, and learning styles. You'll quickly identify the leaders and the followers and you'll be able to see who needs help developing gross motor skills or encouragement joining in. Keep some index cards and a pencil in your pocket. Playtime is a great time to record observations. Share what you learn with parents or caregivers. To learn more about observing and recording children's behavior, see:

Observing Development of the Young Child, Third Edition, by Janice J. Beaty (Macmillan Publishing Company, 1994)

Observing and Recording the Behavior of Young Children, Fourth Edition, by Dorothy Cohen, Virginia Stern, and Nancy Balaban (Teachers College Press, 1996)

Learning to See: Assessment Through Observation by Mary Jane Drummond (Stenhouse Publishers, 1994)

The Power of Observation by Judy R. Jablon, Amy Laura Dombro, and Margo L. Dichtelmiller (Teaching Strategies, Inc., 1999)

Encouraging Participation

Open a door and most children will rush out, eager to play. But some will need your help. Playing together in a large, unstructured environment can be difficult for young children who aren't used to it. They may need encouragement to ask a group of active children, "Can I play, too?"

Sometimes it helps to sit with a shy child and talk about what the others are doing: "Look, Evan is running in front. He's the pirate leader, and they're all pretending to be on an island looking for treasure. Oh, there goes Jeremy, he's shouting that he found it." When the child realizes that all he needs to do is run with the other "pirates," it might make it easier for him to join in.

Dealing With Minor Accidents

Runny noses, tumbles, and scrapes and bruises go hand in hand with outside play. Be prepared by taking first-aid supplies with you. Stash tissues, bandages, and latex gloves in your pocket, just in case. If your school nurse has portable first aid kits, bring one along. For those bumps that inevitably happen when children go too fast and fall, or run into someone else, ice packs work wonders. At the beginning of the year, place small, sealed bags of ice in the school's freezer. When an injured child needs one, send an adult to fetch it. Or, if the child can walk, send him inside with an adult for speedier care. But never leave the group outside without adult supervision.

Chapter 11

Special Events

You've worked hard to create a routine for your students. As a result, they feel confident. They know what to expect from you and each other. They can follow the daily schedule, carry out their jobs, and work independently in centers—all because things pretty much stay the same.

But inevitably there are times when you must interrupt the regular schedule to honor special events such as birthdays, holidays, the arrival of a new student, the birth of a sibling, and the death of a loved one. Here are some ways to recognize those events, without destroying the everyday routines you've established.

Celebrating Birthdays

A birthday is such an important event in a child's life, it deserves to be celebrated at school, with everyone included (especially since most parents are not able to invite all classmates to parties at home).

At the beginning of the year, ask the children to help you make a birthday graph. Instruct each of them to draw a picture on a small square piece of paper. (You might suggest a self-portrait.) At the bottom of the square, write the date of the child's birthday. Then, on a large sheet of poster board, create a graph by listing the months of the year along the left-hand edge. Place the children's drawings in the appropriate columns. This is an easy way to keep track of upcoming birthdays.

A great way to teach math as you keep track of birthdays

To ensure that all children are treated equally on their birthdays, discourage parents from sending in cakes, cupcakes, candy, or other treats, since it only invites comparisons. Some parents will go overboard. Some parents won't send anything at all. Instead, take responsibility for making each birthday memorable and fair. Here are some ways you can create a ritual:

★ **Bake the Cake.** If you have access to an oven, have a small group of students, including the birthday child, bake a cake from scratch or from a mix. It's good to give children choices, such as vanilla or chocolate.

★ **Serve Ice Cream.** If baking a cake is impossible, treat them to ice cream instead. Scoop it into a plastic cup or bowl and place a candle in the center. It makes a special birthday treat for the birthday child. Store ice cream in the cafeteria or teachers' lounge freezer until the celebration.

★ **Encourage Books.** If parents insist on sending something in for the birthday, suggest a new book for the class library. On a bookplate, record the date and the

name of the birthday child.

* **Create a Blue-plate Special.** Bring in a plate from a thrift shop or a set of dishes you no longer use. Use it just for the birthday child's snack. Because it's a one-of-a-kind, it will be very special to the child. Any color will do.

* **Decorate a Birthday Chair.** Invite a small group of children to add ribbons, yarn, balloons, and other trimmings to a chair for the birthday child.

* **Create Cards.** Place folded card stock in the writing center, so children can make cards for the birthday child at work time.

* **Don't Forget Summer Birthdays.** During the last weeks of school, arrange a group celebration for all those with summer birthdays.

Helping Each Other in Difficult Times

Sometimes things happen outside of the classroom that are deeply troubling for children: A grandparent or a pet may die. A parent may be incarcerated. A child may witness violence near or in her home. A chronically ill child may have a frightening trip to the emergency room. There may be a fire in their building. Anything is possible.

Children need to know that they can talk to you about these things. You can reduce some fear and sadness by being open and making it clear that it's okay to share feelings. If the child wants to talk to you, or even seems to want to talk, make the time. You may start with a question, "Nicholas, you look sad. Are you feeling sad today?" If he says, "yes," offer him an ear. "Would you like to sit and tell me why you feel sad?" After he's finished, encourage him to draw and write about the event. Also, ask if he wants to talk about it during meeting to get his classmates' input. If the child is open to this, reassure him that talking together as a group can help. Other children may share similar experiences, which will help the troubled child feel less alone. And even if no one else has had the same experience, the child will feel better knowing he doesn't have to hide his emotions.

Saying Hello and Goodbye

The New Student

Students often join a class after the school year begins or depart before it ends. A

late-arriving child needs support from you and the children to become an active, fully informed member of the group. Here are six ways to make a newcomer feel welcome:

1. Assign a "buddy" to help the new child learn the routines of the classroom.

2. Take extra time to show him around the room, add his name to charts and graphs, and explain where he should store his things.

3. If you have made "special books" for all the children earlier in the year, make one for the new child as soon as possible and read it aloud to the whole group. (See Chapter 2 for details.) It's a great way to make the child feel important and help the others learn things about him.

4. If you did a name study at the beginning of the year, make sure you repeat it for the new child, so that his classmates can learn about his name and draw pictures for his name book. (See Chapter 9.)

5. Add the new child's photo with his name to the photo dictionary in the writing center. (See Chapter 5.) Read the whole book to him, showing him all the other pictures.

6. New children also need help learning the other children's names. At meetings, sing the name songs you sang at the beginning of the year. When you sit with the new child at snack time, tell him the names of the children at the table with him, or have the other children introduce themselves, "Hello, my name is . . ."

It takes time for a new child to feel at home. He may miss his old classroom, teacher, and classmates very much. Allow him to experience those feelings. Offer to help him write a letter to members of his former community. By meeting the child where he is and helping him deal with his feelings, he will, in time, bond with you more deeply.

The Departing Student

If a child must leave before the end of the year, the group needs time to say good-bye. To start the process, have everyone draw a picture for a goodbye book. Mount each child's drawing on construction paper. Sit with the children one by one, and ask what they liked to do with the child who is leaving, or if they have a special memory about her. Write their words on the page opposite their drawing. Bind the book and glue a photograph of the classroom on the front. If possible, get the child's new address so the class can write to her. If you have a class list with addresses and phone numbers, give her a copy so that she can keep in touch with old friends, too.

Keeping Traditional Holidays Under Control

Holidays can be a source of great joy for young children and their teachers. They can also be a source of tremendous stress. Getting a handle on how you will recognize holidays is a good way to nip that stress in the bud. At the beginning of the year, ask the children what they do at home to celebrate holidays throughout the year. Keep in mind that some children don't celebrate any holidays, civic or religious. If that's the case for some of your students, celebrating the holidays at school may make them feel uncomfortable or isolated. You might want to think about creating activities or celebrations that don't focus on specific holidays, so that everyone can participate.

Avoid decorating the classroom for holidays unless everyone celebrates them. Use children's work instead. If your students make presents for their parents at Christmas or Chanukah time, keep them simple.

★ Encourage the children to make cards filled with their own drawing and writing.

★ Give children photos of themselves working in the classroom. They can "frame" them by gluing the images to pieces of cardstock and decorating the edges.

★ If it's customary at your school for teachers to give gifts to children, consider a book for each of them. You can purchase excellent titles from book clubs such as Scholastic's, at very reasonable prices.

Valentine's Day: The Traditional Holiday We Love Most

Valentine's Day is easy to explain to young children. It's the holiday on which we express our feelings to those we love. Therefore, it provides the perfect opportunity for children to make cards for one another and other special people in their lives.

Make sure all class mailboxes are filled to avoid hurt feelings. And don't forget cards for parents and caregivers. Help each child write his home address on an envelope and then take the whole class to the local post office to mail the Valentines. Not only will you teach them an important lesson in writing for real purposes, but you'll also help them share that newfound skill with people they love.

Teacher Tip

Try "The Great Pumpkin Study"

Halloween can be troubling for young children. They may find wearing masks or asking for treats frightening. Instead of focusing on the candy and costumes, create a pumpkin study. Ask the class to help you do the following:

- Find out how much your pumpkin weighs.
- Describe what it looks like on the outside.
- Cut it open to see what's inside.
- Pull out the stringy fibers and save the seeds.
- Plant a few seeds in soil to see if they will grow.

Take the rest of the seeds and toast them. Spread them on a baking sheet in a single layer with a little oil and salt. Bake at 350 degrees until they are browned.

Scrape off the skin, cut the pumpkin flesh into medium-sized pieces, and either boil them in a pot or bake at 350 degrees until soft. Once the pieces cool, you can mash them. Use the cooked pumpkin to make muffins or bread, or just serve it with butter and brown sugar on top.

Creating Your Own Holidays

You don't necessarily need a birthday or a traditional holiday as an excuse to celebrate. You can celebrate the everyday events of life inside your classroom community. Think about your personal photo albums. They're probably filled with reminders of what you and your students have done together. You can create classroom photo albums, too. Children will love poring over old photos, recalling, for example, when they baked their first loaf of bread or went on the trip to the apple orchard. You can also ask children to document class events such as field trips, the arrival of a new student, or the transformation of class caterpillars into butter-flies. Create a book by having each child draw a picture and either write about the

event herself or have you write down her words. Glue each child's drawing to construction paper. Bind the book with staples, metal rings, or by sewing the edge with yarn. On the page opposite the child's drawing write what she said or glue in what she wrote. Place the class books on your library shelves for children to read over and over again. Here are a few more ideas for creating your own "school holidays."

★ **Throw a Party on the Hundredth Day of School.** Many teachers devise ways for children to keep track of days as they progress. A celebration is the perfect way to recognize such conscientious counting.

★ **Celebrate the Children's Hard Work.** After taking four trips to the local art museum, one teacher helped her children display their own drawings, paintings, collages, clay sculptures, and murals in their own "Kindergarten Museum." The art was placed on classroom walls along with biographical information about each artist. The children created an invitation for their "art opening" and sent them to their parents and school administrators. On the day of the opening, they served cookies that they baked.

★ **Host Seasonal Sing-a-longs.** Teach the children songs that celebrate autumn, winter, spring, and summer. It's an effective, fun way to teach about the seasons. Make sure the children know all the words, and then invite parents and family members to attend a sing-along. Hand out song sheets so guests can participate, too.

★ **Say Thanks!** If a group of older students volunteered regularly in your classroom, show your gratitude by hosting a pizza party in their honor. Ask your children to make thank-you cards for the volunteers as well.

Moving children from a special celebration to the end-of-the-day meeting may not be easy, but it's the best way to reintroduce them to their routine. Have them sing a familiar song as they gather on the rug. This will serve as an incentive. The simple act of coming together again will also send an important message: Today was different and fun, but now it's back to normal. Our school day has an orderly flow.

Chapter 12

End-of-the-Day Meeting

It's mid-afternoon, time to get ready to go home. So, gather the children on the rug for the final meeting of the day. If they've been working independently, they'll want to discuss what they've done. You may need to talk to them about a notice to parents explaining a field trip, a school event, or any number of things. And finally, you and the children need to say goodbye.

Once you've created a sense of community in your classroom, it might be hard for children to leave it. After all, they've had fun, felt safe, and learned so much. The idea of leaving may make some of them anxious. So coming together as a group, talking about the day's events, and planning for tomorrow reminds children that they will return.

Summing Up the Day

When everyone is on the rug, you could begin by reading a short story. A story can help settle the group and gives you another chance to share a favorite piece of children's literature with them. If there isn't time for a story, you might read a poem or lead one more song.

You can also have children report daily news. Ask them to suggest significant events that should be entered on the calendar. For example, "Thomas built a really tall building in the block area," "Adrienne held the rabbit for the first time," "Jeanine, Michael, and Emilio made muffins for snack time." The day's "news reporter" decides on the one item to record for the day.

If you're teaching four-year-olds, you should write the news reporter's choice exactly as the children tell you. But if you have older children who are able to write, you may let the news reporter take the pen.

Ask the whole group to listen carefully and tell you what letters correspond to the sounds they hear as you write the news for all to see on a piece of chart paper. For

Sunday	Monday	Tuesday	Wednesday	Thursday	Friday	Saturday
No School [1]	**No School** [2]	**No School** [3]	WC HCClb VZ+rC. [4]	Today we gt bcs. [5]	We flt rbct V grf. [6]	**No School** [7]
No School [8]	We T cprs [9]	We cRbt fdns a kag. [10]	**No School** [11]	**No School** [12]	**No School** [13]	**No School** [14]
No School [15]	vce got a rbt. [16]	WehDA F FIRD Rl [17]	Welt r Tqb wert r robt [18]	We rd slesle. [19]	Sa WMS WR cls. [20]	**No School** [21]
No School [22]	We hd SMI grps [23]	We dd r kinbr. [24]	We dd cntrs. [25]	**No School** [26]	**No School** [27]	**No School** [28]
No School [29]	WErApp Krn. [30]					**No School**

> *Charting daily news together gives you an opportunity to model writing.*

example, if the news reporter instructs you to write, "Today we played outside," write only what the class hears. It might look like this:

Today (A child saw the word on the morning chart and spelled it.)

we (Children heard the sounds for *w* and *e*.)

plad (Children heard the sounds for *p*,*l*,*a*, and *d*.)

otsid (Children heard the sounds for *o*,*t*,*s*,*i*, and *d*.)

Instead of showing the children the "correct" way to spell each word, accept what they tell you. By using developmental spelling like this, you give the children an important message: It's okay to write only the letters for the sounds you hear. Children are more likely to listen for and write sounds in words they want to write if they see you doing it, too.

The children have listened for sounds, and you've written what they've heard. They probably came closer to the correct spelling than the news reporter would have on her own because they pooled their knowledge. You've modeled how to form the letters by writing them on the chart. Now the news reporter can do her job, copy what's on the chart onto the monthly calendar.

Teacher Tip

Compile a Class News Big Book

At the end of each month, cover the filled calendar page with clear contact paper, punch three holes in the side, and add it to *Our Class News* big book. Use metal rings to hold the pages together. Children will love flipping through the book and remembering the "good old days."

Assigning "Homework"

After discussing all the daily news that's fit to print, turn to the subject of the next day. If the children are going on a trip and need to return permission slips, remind them. If you have a note for them to take home to parents, tell them about it.

If your school district insists on "homework" for kindergarten, you'll need a system for sending and receiving it. A two-pocket, 8 ½-by-11-inch folder for each student

works well. In one pocket, place homework that is to be completed and returned. In the other pocket, place school work the child accomplished that day, the previous day's corrected homework, notes to the parents, and any administrative messages.

Instead of a two-pocket folder, Lenore Furman uses a small, softcover notebook for each of her kindergarten children. In it, she writes notes to the child's parents, making sure that they understand how they can help. These notebooks also enable her to individualize the homework. Children who are still struggling to write single words may be asked to practice their names as homework, while those who are reading sentences may be asked to write some sentences using words they know. They can then read their sentences to their parents and practice writing high-frequency words such as *the, he, she, it, am,* and so forth.

The best homework for young children is listening to stories read aloud by their parents or family members. Encourage children to borrow books from the classroom lending library so that their caregivers will have high-quality, self-chosen picture books to read.

Teacher Tip

Establish a Lending Library

Create a home lending library by collecting inexpensive, quality picture books. Use your bonus points from book clubs, ask parents for donations, and frequent garage sales and flea markets to find good children's books. Place a pocket and card in each book. When a child wants to take a book home, just write the name on the card and put it in a special place so you'll know who has which book. You could also attach library pockets, one for each child, to a piece of heavy chart paper. When a child takes a book, she puts its card in her pocket. When she returns the book, she takes the card from her pocket, places it back into the book, and puts the book back on the lending library shelves.

Encourage families to keep a log. Use the reproducible form or lined paper for listing the books they read together. (See Appendix.) Alongside each book's title, the child can indicate how much he liked it: "not at all," "a little," "a lot," or "the best!"

Another collaborative form of homework is cooking. Send home copies of recipes from school and encourage parents to let children take the lead in preparing them. By watching their children recreate their culinary masterpieces, parents will see the skills they are acquiring in school.

The end-of-the-day meeting is a good time for children to "show and tell" projects they've done at home with their parents. They may have cooked something special, planted a garden, or conducted a simple experiment. Ask the child what he and his family member did first, second, and third. That way, you limit "show and tell" to

things children have done, rather than to things they have, thereby stemming competition over possessions.

Just as some children need security objects from home to help them feel safe at school, some children need security objects from school to help them feel comfortable about leaving. Some teachers use a class mascot, usually a stuffed animal, that travels to a different child's home each night. Place the mascot in a backpack and include a journal and pen. At home, the child and parent can write about the mascot's adventures during its stay with them. The next day, read the journal entry at morning meeting. Over the course of the year, each child will have many chances to take the mascot home.

> Dear Parents,
>
> Children who like reading have usually developed a love for stories and books early in their lives. I have established a lending library so your child can enjoy some of his/her favorite stories at home.
>
> As part of your child's homework, please read the story to him/her. Then complete the Monthly Reading Log. Please return the book and the reading log to school the next day.
>
> Books will be sent home Monday through Thursday. Please ensure that your child brings his/her bookbag to school everyday. This will help protect our books.
>
> I hope you and your child find this special reading time pleasurable and will set aside time each day to enjoy a good book.
>
> Sincerely,
> Ms. Furman

Keeping Dismissal Calm

Dismissal produces natural anxieties in children. "Will my mom be on time?" "What bus do I get on?" "What if I'm too scared to go on a play date at my friend's house?" Any of these questions could be swirling around in a child's head.

Anxieties will disintegrate over time, though, if the dismissal is predictable from day one. Children need to know the routine in order to become confident. They also need to know that you are watching out for them. Because you have many children, you need a system that allows you to answer questions and say goodbye to each one individually.

Begin your routine by sending a few children at a time to collect their belongings and asking them to return to the rug when they have everything. You might say:

★ If your name begins with the letter *M* or the sound /b/, get your things.

★ If you are wearing stripes today, get your things.

★ If you have an *R* anywhere in your name, get your things.

Directions like these help develop children's classification skills. They also ensure a steady, efficient flow of children to and from the coat and backpack area.

If adults come to your classroom to pick up the children, have them check parent

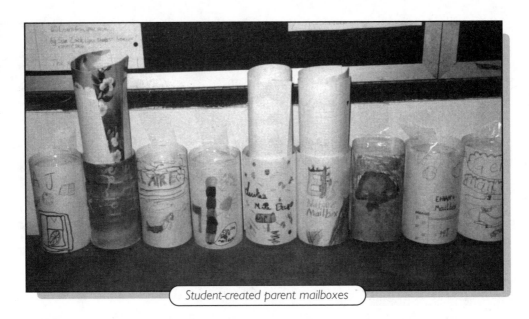

Student-created parent mailboxes

mailboxes for any notes. If space permits, position these mailboxes immediately outside the classroom or just inside near the door. Some teachers use hanging shoe storage bags—made of vinyl and designed to hang from door tops—to create mailboxes.

Other teachers use plastic quart containers. They line them up next to one another on a shelf, write each child's name on them, and arrange them on top of the cubbies.

Whatever kind of mailboxes you use, show adults where they are, and remind them to check them each day. For children who are not picked up by parents, however, the homework folder is best for sending home notes and other forms of correspondence.

Your school's voice mail system is another way to keep parents informed. Give each parent your school phone number. Every Monday, record a message about the upcoming week. You can also describe briefly any curriculum changes and make requests for donations, such as healthy snack foods. Parents can simply listen to your message and hang up, or leave a message of their own. This simple procedure can greatly enhance communication between home and school.

Before children leave your classroom, make sure you see and say goodbye to the person who is scheduled to pick them up. That way, you will know that each child is safe. It will also give you a chance to speak briefly with parents about things that happened during the day.

Be sure to keep a list handy that lets you and the other teachers know who is authorized to pick up children. At most schools, parents provide this information at the beginning of the year.

Chapter 13

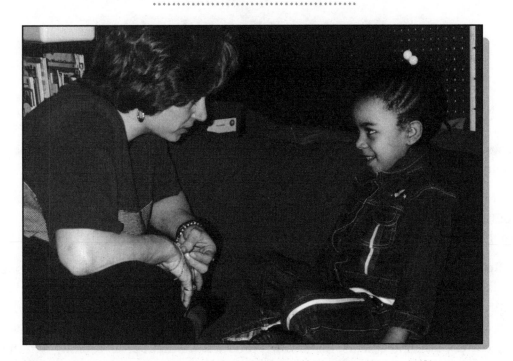

End of the Year

By the end of the year, classroom life should be humming along because you've taught children the routines they need to work independently and collaboratively. They've learned how to get along and learn from one another.

Although we may assume that the thought of summer vacation excites all children, it can trigger worry in some. Because they've enjoyed such a great deal of time with you, and have become more confident, independent, and happy in the process, many children don't want to leave school. To them, the prospect of breaking from work means breaking from daily opportunities to play with friends in a safe, stimulating environment.

But there are ways to ease children's anxieties by helping them to hold onto all the wonderful experiences they've had.

Sharing What They've Accomplished

Start by taking frequent trips down memory lane. Help children recall all the things they did during the year. Reread class books that you've made, such as the *Our Class News* big book. Ask the children to think back to the first days of school and talk about what they were like.

Giving each child a handmade book is a meaningful gesture and serves a purpose: Your gift can be revisited over and over again during the summer, when a child wants to remember his school experience. Here are three ideas:

★ **Recipes du Jour.** If cooking has been a regular part of your curriculum, compile a class cookbook. If you've been compiling recipes throughout the year, assembling them into a book shouldn't be that difficult. If you haven't, go back and copy the recipes you've used in class. Allow space on each page so the children can draw pictures of the ingredients, the finished products, or themselves cooking. On the first page, include a note to the parents explaining how you've helped the children measure, mix, stir, crush, crack, and blend. Also, invite parents to try out the recipes with their children during the summer months.

★ **Goodbye, Farewell, Adios, Adieu.** Make *Goodbye Books* for each child. Gather photos of the children at work in the classroom. Fold construction paper into a book, and glue a photo to each page. If you know who the child's next teacher will be, include a photo of her as well. Then create captions by asking them to write something themselves or by telling you what to write beneath each picture.

Goodbye Books, filled with personal memories and photos of the year, make wonderful keepsakes.

★ **"Every Picture Tells a Story" Book.** Children love to commemorate events by drawing pictures. Compiling their masterpieces into a book makes a great going-away gift. Ask children to create a special end-of-year pencil drawing on a piece of white paper, and be sure to include their names. Photocopy each child's drawing onto card stock or glue copies onto colored pieces of construction paper. Bind the drawings together into a book.

Talking About What They'll Do

You may also want to talk with the children about the future—what they'll be doing over the summer and what they know about their next grade. Discussing the past, present, and future helps young children grasp the concept of time passing. Summer may hold frightening uncertainties, but perhaps last fall did, too, and the children were fine. Remind them of that.

A graph that illustrates children's summer activities and a directory of their summer contact information are good tools for getting them to visualize the future and plan ahead. Parents will particularly appreciate the directory so that their children can stay in touch with friends over vacation.

To ease children's anxiety about the coming school year, arrange for visits to the classrooms they'll be attending. Invite their future teachers to visit your classroom as well. Before they arrive, help the children think of questions. Their teachers will be able to reassure them that although some things may be different next year, many things will be similar.

End-of-Year Celebrations

Two to three weeks before the end of school, host one big party for all the children who have summer birthdays. Involve everyone in baking the cake, decorating the chairs, or setting up. Basically, whatever you've done for the other children, make sure you do it for these children as well.

Also, think about a large year-end event, such as a picnic. Hold it during the school day or, better yet, early evening so families can come. Try to find a local park or playground where the children can run and play together. The parents will be thrilled to see how well their children have learned to get along.

Making it a family event also gives you a chance to talk informally with parents. You've worked hard all year to create a solid bond between the families and the classroom. You've sent home newsletters, notes, and work documenting their children's growth. You've encouraged parents to contribute to classroom life in many ways. You've asked them for help when you've been concerned about their children. Celebrating a successful year with them is a good way to say thank you.

There are also ways to celebrate the work the children have done. As you empty files and portfolios, and remove things from the walls, show the work to the whole group. And send it home well before the last day of school so you won't be preoccupied with clean up on the last day.

Once you take the children's work off the walls, the room could wind up looking pretty barren, so hang up photos of the children or group projects they've done. Also, put class books out on shelves. This will encourage them to reflect on all they've accomplished and learned.

The Final Day

Keep the last day low key. Avoid an elaborate party, which will only consume your time and attention. Instead, just "hang out" with the children. Make time to talk with each one individually. Give them their handmade books, perhaps, and talk about how much you've enjoyed the year together: "Kristen, here is your goodbye book. It tells a story about your time in school this year. It was fun being your teacher, Kristen. You always made me smile. Remember, you can read your goodbye book whenever you want to see me or your friends at school." If you will not be back in the fall, tell the children what you will be doing. And if you will be back, let them know that they can come to visit you.

When the children file out for the last time, keep in mind it's okay to cry. Saying goodbye is a big deal. You've cared for these children for nearly a year. You've done your best for each of them. They've crawled into your heart—and now you have to let them go. There's not a teacher we know who doesn't feel sad.

As you look ahead to some well-deserved rest, remember the lessons you've learned, for they will help you create an even stronger community of learners next year. Learning how to be a teacher never ends. Future students will always bring new challenges. Remember that good routines and predictable schedules will go a long way toward helping you meet them.

Arrival Activities

Meeting

Classroom Routines That Really Work for Pre-K and Kindergarten Scholastic Professional Books

Once upon a time there was a big cow.

Story

MILK

Lunch

Rest

Outside Play

Classroom Routines That Really Work for Pre-K and Kindergarten Scholastic Professional Books

Work Centers

Snack

Classroom Routines That Really Work for Pre-K and Kindergarten Scholastic Professional Books

Date _____

Center Choices Checklist

Child	Mon.	Tues.	Wed.	Thurs.	Fri.
1.					
2.					
3.					
4.					
5.					
6.					
7.					
8.					
9.					
10.					
11.					
12.					
13.					
14.					
15.					
16.					
17.					
18.					
19.					
20.					
21.					
22.					
23.					
24.					
25.					

Explanation of use appears on page 43.

Write around the room.

Name

Name _____

Write the numbers   Trace the numbers

Which number won?

			Write the numbers	Trace the numbers
			12	12
			11	11
			10	10
			9	9
			8	8
			7	7
			6	6
			5	5
			4	4
			3	3
			2	2

Racing Dice (for use with two dice)

Explanation of use appears on page 71.

Classroom Routines That Really Work for Pre-K and Kindergarten Scholastic Professional Books

Which number won? □

1	2	3	4	5	6
1	2	3	4	5	6
1	2	3	4	5	6
1	2	3	4	5	6
1	2	3	4	5	6

Write the numbers

Trace the numbers

Name

Explanation of use appears on page 71.
Classroom Routines That Really Work for Pre-K and Kindergarten
Scholastic Professional Books

Racing Dice

(for use with one die)

Science Observation

Name _____ Date _____

Draw and write what you noticed today.

_____

_____

_____

_____

Classroom Routines That Really Work for Pre-K and Kindergarten Scholastic Professional Books

Snack Request Form

_____

We need the following item for our snack program:

_____

Please send the item by _____ .

If you are unable to provide this item, please let me know.
Thank you for your continued support and cooperation.

Sincerely,

Snack Request Form

_____

We need the following item for our snack program:

_____

Please send the item by _____ .

If you are unable to provide this item, please let me know.
Thank you for your continued support and cooperation.

Sincerely,

Classroom Routines That Really Work for Pre-K and Kindergarten Scholastic Professional Books

Monthly Home Reading Log

Child's Name _____

	Title of Book	Date	Who read the story?
1.			
2.			
3.			
4.			
5.			
6.			
7.			
8.			
9.			
10.			
11.			
12.			
13.			
14.			
15.			
16.			
17.			
18.			
19.			
20.			

Explanation of use appears on page 110.